HOW TO WRITE
PSYCHOLOGY
PAPERS

HOW TO WRITE PSYCHOLOGY PAPERS

SECOND EDITION

Les Parrott III

Seattle Pacific University

BF
76.5
P27
1999

 LONGMAN

An Imprint of Addison Wesley Longman, Inc.

New York • Reading, Massachusetts • Menlo Park, California • Harlow, England
Don Mills, Ontario • Sydney • Mexico City • Madrid • Amsterdam

Editor-in-Chief: Priscilla McGeehon
Acquisitions Editor: Eric Stano
Marketing Manager: Anne Wise
Project Manager: Dora Rizzuto
Design Manager and Cover Designer: John Callahan
Cover Photo: PhotoDisc, Inc.
Prepress Services Supervisor: Valerie A. Vargas
Electronic Production Specialist: Joanne Del Ben
Print Buyer: Denise Sandler
Electronic Page Makeup: Tim Roberts
Printer and Binder: Maple-Vail
Cover Printer: Coral Graphic Services, Inc.

Library of Congress Cataloging-in-Publication Data

Parrott, Les.
    How to write psychology papers / Les Parrott III. — 2nd ed.
      p.   cm.
    Includes bibliographical references and index.
    ISBN 0-321-04466-5
    1. Psychology—Research—Methodology. 2. Psychology--Study and
teaching (Higher)   I. Title.
    BF76.5.P27 1999   98-27536
    808'.06615—dc21   CIP

Please visit our website at http://longman.awl.com

ISBN 0-321-04466-5

2345678910—MA—01009998

To my students

CONTENTS

PREFACE

WILLIAM of Occam, who lived in England more than 600 years ago, was a graduate of Oxford. He was an intelligent man who sharpened his mind by learning how to cut to the core of any issue. He became famous for his method of thinking, known as Occam's Razor. It separates the essentials from the nonessentials. It removes all unnecessary elements to expose a subject's essence.

How to Write Psychology Papers was written with Occam's Razor in mind. In these pages I present the bare bones, the essential tools, for writing psychology papers. The book can be read quickly on one's own or as a supplement in a psychology course. I wrote this book after teaching hundreds of bright and motivated students who needed a "coach" to teach them — step by step — the skills of writing psychology papers. They had the ball, but needed direction on how to run and which way to go.

The 1929 Rose Bowl game is notorious among sports enthusiasts. It is known as football's "Wrongest Run." California was leading Georgia Tech, 7 to 6, when Roy Riegels became confused and ran the ball the length of the gridiron toward his opponent's goal. The crowd roared in amazement, "Stop! Stop!" The noise was so great Riegels thought the crowd was cheering him on. He ran with more and more passion, not realizing he was headed in the wrong direction.

The young athlete memorized his team's plays, he practiced routinely, and he trained diligently as a football player. But without a clear sense of direction, "Wrong-Way Riegels" lost the game for his team.

When it comes to writing papers, some psychology majors are in danger of being like this unfortunate athlete. They study, research, and write with zeal but do not see the big picture. They work hard and still miss the goal.

Think of *How to Write Psychology Papers* as your personal trainer — a coach who keeps you running in the right direction. Even gold-medal athletes need a coach. The same is true of bright students. Without direction from a knowledgeable coach, hardworking students can lose the benefits of their efforts.

How to Write Psychology Papers can be read completely through and then used later as a ready and simple reference. Mark it up and keep it handy. Use its table of contents and index to look up specific points of interest. Its chapters are short and can be used as capsule summaries of specific writing concerns.

Several individuals provided valuable feedback on the many drafts of this text. Those deserving special thanks include Travis Jeremiah, Manny Joe, Joy Hammersla, Doug Henning, Don MacDonald, Delbert McHenery, Leslie Parrott, Mike Roe, Steve Scott, Carole Wade, and Jim Waller. Each of these persons has read the manuscript as a whole or large parts of it. They gave feedback on style as well as substance, and the book is stronger because of their useful advice. Daniel Liestman, bibliographic specialist for the social sciences at Seattle Pacific University, helped significantly with chapters 5 and 6. I am indebted to him for sharing his expertise. Heidi Chavez at Addison Wesley Longman gave this project vision and helped refine my approach. The tough-minded suggestions from the reviewers commissioned by Addison Wesley Longman were also extremely beneficial. Thank you all.

LES PARROTT III

About the Author

Les Parrott III is an associate professor of clinical psychology and co-director of the Center for Relationship Development at Seattle Pacific University. He is the author of numerous articles and books, including *Counseling and Psychotherapy* (McGraw-Hill), *Helping the Struggling Adolescent* (Zondervan), *High-Maintenance Relationships* (Tyndale), and the award-winning *Saving Your Marriage Before it Starts* (Zondervan).

PART ONE

BECOMING A BETTER WRITER

OVERCOMING PAPER PANIC

I love writing. I love the swirl and swing of words as they tangle with human emotions.
— *James Michener*

I have always been able to gain my living without doing any work; for the writing of books and magazine matter was always play, not work. I enjoyed it; it was merely billiards to me.
— *Mark Twain*

YOUR professor distributes the syllabus and describes the course. All is fine until she mentions the words *term paper*. You are struck with a thud in your gut. "A minimum of 15 pages is required," she declares. Your heart races. "Be sure to use APA style," she continues. You feel your palms begin to sweat. You have visions of becoming lost in the library stacks. What's worse, you know the panic will only increase when it comes time actually to write.

If you relate to this scenario, take heart. You're not alone. Only people like James Michener love the "swirl and swing of words"; only people like Mark Twain equate writing with playing pool. Most people dread having to construct a cogent sentence or write a thoughtful paragraph.

Writing is tough. Even William F. Buckley, author of more than a dozen books, said, "I do not like to write, for the simple reason that writing is extremely hard work." William Zinsser has said, "I don't like to write, but I take great pleasure in having written."

Writing term papers, however, does not need to be painful. David McClelland, a Harvard psychology professor, made a startling discovery in the 1960s. Through testing, he accurately predicted which college students would be most successful. The determining factor was not SAT scores or the students' GPAs, however, but the way these students used their minds. McClelland's research also demonstrated that all students could *learn* to use their minds in ways that high achievers do (Walter & Siebert, 1990). And there's more good news. It doesn't take long to learn how to think in ways that will make you more successful as a student — especially when it comes to writing papers.

Three qualities are crucially important in combating paper panic:

- First, you have to *want* to learn how to write papers.
- Second, you must identify what obstacles stand in the way of your learning how to write papers.
- Third, you must consult knowledgeable resources for information that will show you how to overcome the obstacles on your path to becoming an effective writer.

That's all there is to it!

Since you are reading this book, you are already well on your way to writing excellent psychology papers. You certainly have the desire, and this book will help you to identify roadblocks and help you to overcome them.

So if you suffer from panic when you hear the words *term paper, literature review, empirical paper, essay* or *research proposal*, relax. Take a deep breath and rely on this book to guide you in your journey toward writing quality papers. Who knows, you might even learn to love the swirl and swing of words.

CHAPTER 2

TOOLS OF THE WRITER'S TRADE

ONE of the most unimaginable feats I have ever witnessed was a person at the Los Angeles County fair who wrote in miniature. With a fine pen, a microscope, and lots of patience, he printed Lincoln's Gettysburg Address — all 268 words — on a human hair less than 3 inches in length.

I am not advocating that you write your next term paper on a few strands of hair, but that man's miniature writing reminded me of the importance of proper writing tools. Even when the goal is simply getting words on an ordinary sheet of paper, a writer needs the proper equipment, supplies, and environment.

A writer's tools include anything that makes writing easier. "The tools I need for my work," said William Faulkner, "are paper, tobacco, food and a little whiskey." Mickey Spillane said, "The typewriter's my carpenter box." "All I needed," said Agatha Christie, "was a steady table and a typewriter." Writers' tools are often unique to their preferences and quirks. John Steinbeck said, "Pencils must be round. A hexagonal pencil cuts my fingers after a long day." In this chapter I will note some of the most commonly used writing aids. If they help you, great. If not, try a round pencil.

WRITING MACHINES

In 1876, Mark Twain took advantage of a recent invention. He was the first to write a book, *The Adventures of Tom Sawyer*, using a modern gadget known as "the Type-Writer." Time passed and typewriters became one word. They also became portable and electric (Schultz, 1990).

In the late 1970s, about 100 years after Tom Sawyer, writers began to talk about "disks," "memory," "software," and "megabytes." Today, the personal computer (PC) and its word processing software have virtually replaced electronic typewriters as the essential tool for contemporary writers. With the mere touch of a few keys on a PC keyboard, one can quickly and easily move entire paragraphs, add a footnote, alphabetize a list, or build an index. There are dozens of computer packages with a wide price range. But if money prohibits you from owning a PC, it need not keep you from using one. Most universities have computer centers fully equipped for student use.

If you are not already experienced in using a word processor, you will want to learn the rudimentary skills as soon as you can. It will save you countless hours of tedious rewriting chores. Many systems, for example, will automatically flag grammar, style, spelling, and usage errors electronically. Some can even calculate reading levels and make recommendations. As we will see later, however, these high-tech tools cannot be a substitute for personal spelling, punctuation, and grammar skills.

THE WRITER'S BOOKSHELF

There are a number of books, such as the *Publication Manual of the American Psychological Association*, to which any serious psychology writer should have ready access. I will discuss these later. Here, however, I want to recommend a few volumes that belong on the shelf of *every* writer.

Writing without a dictionary is like playing basketball without a backboard. Dictionaries give writers an edge. They guide the writer's work and make it easier. You would expect every dictionary to define the same words in the same way. They don't. Some dictionaries list the most current or dominant meaning; some provide definitions in historical order. Some stick to the basics while others seem obsessed with minutiae. The question is which is best for you. If you call on your dictionary just to confirm your recollection, a paperback version may do. If you have a real need to make distinctions, you're better off with a solid hardcover volume such as *American Heritage, Merriam Webster's Collegiate, Random House,* or *Webster's New World*. But never use a word you don't fully understand.

When you are looking for just the right word and need some help, a good thesaurus becomes a treasure trove. Most are organized like a dictionary. You look up a word and it supplies you with a list of related words and phrases. Some of the most commonly used include *The New Roget's Thesaurus, The Doubleday Roget's Thesaurus,* and *Webster's Collegiate Thesaurus*. When you want to express your ideas fully you'll find a thesaurus invaluable — essential, profitable, priceless, efficacious. . . .

"A well-placed quotation," according to James Charlton, author of *The Writer's Quotation Book*, "lends weight to one's own opinion by somehow invoking a higher authority." I agree. If you have the cash, pick up *Bartlett's Familiar Quotations* or *The Oxford Dictionary of Quotations*. They are two of the best.

THE WRITER'S ENVIRONMENT

I know of a writer in Paris who rented desk space in the restaurant on the first landing stage of the Eiffel Tower. A friend found him there, typing away contentedly on a story.

"Well," said the friend, "you certainly must be attached to the Eiffel Tower!"

"Attached to it!" snorted the writer. "This is the only place in Paris where I can avoid seeing that thing!"

Writers need space free from distractions. Few writers enjoy the luxury of a spacious study lined with oak-paneled walls, bookshelves, highback leather chairs, and a crackling fire. Most writers make do with a small, carved-out space that is amazingly conducive to productivity.

Far too many students work at a temporary desk, spreading out papers, getting organized, and then packing it all up every time the table is used for something else. Countless hours are lost tracking down mislaid papers and books.

Save yourself time and frustration by securing a consistent place to study and write. It may be a desk in your dormitory room or in a reserved library study carrel. I like it simple: a well-lighted room, a clean desk top, a bulletin board, a bookcase, and a file drawer. I have a colleague who writes at a computer tucked in a small closet. Every writer is different. What's important is that your writing environment be relatively comfortable, and that it helps you slay the monster of writer's block. Don't delay setting up your own writing area. It will improve your efficiency and bring you closer to writing successful papers.

CHAPTER 3

THE SECRET TO SUCCESSFUL WRITING

EVER since sending away for my Captain Decoder ring in the third grade, I have loved secrets. The mystery of sending secret information to an "undercover" friend was thrilling. But there are many secrets I'm glad have been uncovered.

Ice cream is an example. The chefs of Europe tried to keep the recipe for ice cream a secret. They wanted to reserve the delicious dessert for kings and nobility. Aren't you glad they failed?

The secret to successful writing is open to everyone. Surprisingly, it does not involve *aptitude* or *talent*. These factors, reflected by GPA, IQ, and SAT scores, are honored by college admission personnel, but rigorous research reveals they are not the best predictors of academic success.

THE SECRET OF BEING

Dr. Martin Seligman, a psychology professor at the University of Pennsylvania and the author of *Learned Optimism* (1990), has shown that *attitude* is a fundamental yet little known key to academic success. Students who believe they can and will succeed *are* more likely to reach their goals. Optimists get better grades than their SATs predict; pessimists get worse grades then their SATs predict.

The first experiment leading to this discovery involved two groups of dogs that were given mild shocks to their feet (the kind you feel when you touch a doorknob on a dry winter day). One group was able to escape the shock by leaping over a low barrier into another section of the box. The other group was restrained in harnesses that made it impossible to escape the jolt. After only a few trials, both groups were put in a situation where they could escape easily. They were again shocked. The group that had originally been harnessed did not try to escape when they had the chance. They made no effort to escape! They just whined and lay down in the experimental chamber — resigned to a fate they had come to believe they could not control. They had learned that nothing they did mattered, so why try!

The implications of this study were glaring to Dr. Seligman. If dogs could learn something as complex as the futility of their actions, imagine how similar experiences affect humans. Seligman and his colleagues have conducted numerous experiments since this first one and have shown that helplessness and pessimism clearly produce similar results in both animals and humans.

College students who have never been affirmed for their writing are a good example. When they face another writing assignment, they either give up or make only halfhearted attempts to accomplish their goal — even when they have everything it takes to succeed at writing a quality paper.

A bad paper is like the "one that got away" to the person who fishes. Optimistic students never look back but find ways to believe in themselves and the next opportunity. The key to overcoming helplessness and unlocking your optimism is to change your "explanatory style." What Seligman means by this is changing how you explain to yourself the bad things (such as receiving a low grade on a paper) that happen to you. Students who give up easily habitually say something like "It's me, it's going to last forever, it's going to undermine everything I do." Others, those who resist giving in to misfortune, say "It was just circumstances, it's going away quickly anyway, and, besides, there's much more in life." According to Seligman, "Your explanatory style stems directly from your view of your place in the world — whether you think you are valuable and deserving, or worthless and hopeless" (Seligman, 1990, p. 44). One of the first secrets to successful writing is believing you can and will succeed.

THE SECRET OF DOING

There is a second secret to successful writing. It is found in harnessing your time and energy. No one has enough time. There are too many things to do and too many tasks without limits. A term paper on the role of women in psychology, for example, could easily be developed into an entire book. Successful writing means organizing, planning, and focusing your attention on the task at hand.

When a writing assignment seems threatening, your number-one enemy is procrastination. It can destroy you. William James said, "Nothing is so fatiguing as the eternal hanging on of an uncompleted task." There is an imp in each of us that wants to rebel against work. An uncomfortable chair, a pencil that is too short, a book that is not available, and 100 other things can deceptively excuse us from getting started. Among the most common excuses are (1) "I don't have enough time now," (2) "I'm in the wrong place — it's too noisy, etc.," (3) "Other things are more important," and (4) "I'm not in the right mood" (Klauser, 1987). We can be armed with the best of intentions, yet we are unable to begin. "When I'm supposed to be writing," says author Fran Lebowitz, "I clean my apartment, take my clothes to the laundry, get organized, make lists, do the dishes. I would never do a dish unless I had to write."

Procrastination can be beaten by doing something NOW! Lao-tse, a Chinese philosopher, said, "The journey of a thousand miles begins with the first step." If the idea of a ten-page paper is frightening, break it down into manageable segments. Don't try to live an entire semester at a time. Concentrate on phases by setting small goals that will ultimately bring you to your destination. If you are paralyzed by indecision on a project, set a time by which you'll make the decision. Make the decision at that time, and immediately begin work on the project. Warning: You may end up enjoying it. Erasmus said, "The desire to write grows with writing." Do it now!

Some students procrastinate because they mistakenly believe they are writing in stone. If you are stuck, write whatever comes out and lower your expectation for the first draft. Even professional writers produce first drafts that are entirely unacceptable for publication. "I have rewritten, often several times, every work I have ever published," says Vladimir Nabokov. "My pencils outlast their erasers." So begin. Not the entire paper. Just the first paragraph. Then continue.

David Schmitt (1992), in his helpful book *The Winning Edge*, provides the following suggestions for overcoming procrastination and beating writer's block:

- Don't wait for inspiration. Follow the DO IT NOW principle.
- Write the easiest parts first.
- Begin each writing session by revising what you wrote last time.
- Set clear writing goals on your schedule.
- Avoid "one best way" thinking and realize that there is never a *perfect* way to organize your paper.
- Don't get down on yourself if you are stuck. Even the most experienced writers sometimes get writer's block.
- Develop a positive attitude by saying to yourself such things as: "I can handle this project" (Schmitt, 1992, p. 239).

I would add one more suggestion to this list: Don't waste time searching the Internet. While the Net can be a valuable tool for finding information and making connections when one is disciplined, it becomes a collosal time waster for the procrastinating student (see Chapter 6 for tips on how to use the Internet effectively and efficiently in research).

The secret to successful writing? It's found in being an optimist and putting action behind your planning. Perhaps it is even more simple. When Guy de Maupassant was asked the secret to successful writing, he said, "Get black on white."

PART TWO

THE WRITING PROCESS

CHOOSING A TOPIC

A FRIEND of mine took his 7-year-old son on a sight-seeing tour of Washington, DC. They explored the Capitol, the Lincoln Memorial, and the Air and Space Museum. When they got to the Washington Monument the missile-minded youngster stared and said, "They'll never get it off the ground."

Some college students feel the same way about writing psychology papers. The weight of a term paper assignment can feel as if it will never get off the ground.

Getting airborne on a writing assignment begins with choosing a topic — a *specific* topic. Most students need to narrow their writing topics more than they imagine.

Behaviorism may be a fascinating and important subject, but a 5- to 15-page paper can barely scratch its surface. It is much better to pin down a narrow, more manageable topic such as the early history of behaviorism or behavioral treatment strategies with depressed adolescents.

In trying to narrow a broad subject for a term paper, ask yourself what interests you most about the topic. For example, which particular aspect of behaviorism is most fascinating to you? Is there a part of behaviorism you would especially like to learn more about? What about extinction, shaping, or negative reinforcement? Are you interested in knowing how positive reinforcement influences children's school performance? The goal is to slice out a narrow wedge from the larger subject.

You can narrow a subject to a manageable size by focusing on a particular age group — infants, adolescents, or retirees, for example. You can limit a topic by focusing on racial or ethnic groups such as African-Americans or Asian-Americans. You might limit a topic by means of a theoretical approach such as Freudian or humanistic. Other possibilities include geographical area, gender, time frame, outcomes, and so on. Limiting a topic depends on your purpose in writing the paper.

Give it a try. How would you narrow the subject of schizophrenia? Before you read on, write down a few manageable examples:

_____

_____

_____

_____

There are no right or wrong answers, but here are some suggestions: the biological causes of schizophrenia, biomedical causes of schizophrenia, psychological treatments for schizophrenia, coping strategies of family members with a paranoid schizophrenic, and so on.

Try one more. Narrow the subject of adolescents. Write down your ideas:

_____

_____

_____

_____

Here are some more suggestions for narrowing the subject of adolescents: cognitive development in early adolescence, impediments to moral development in adolescents, the influence of television on adolescent values, adolescent sex roles, adolescents at risk for alcoholism, and so on.

Once you have narrowed your subject, the next concern is whether the topic lends itself to research. Are there books, articles, documents, and other materials available? It might be interesting to do a comparative study on the role of the world's major religions and the psychological role of music in worship, but chances are that what is written on the topic may not be plentiful or easily accessible. If you have four weeks and five pages, your topic must match these limitations.

Here are some "dos and don'ts" that can help you choose a term paper topic that will receive high marks:

- Talk with classmates about their paper ideas to help ignite your thinking about your own topic.
- Scan the tables of contents and indexes of textbooks as well as class notes for ideas.
- Scan periodical indexes (discussed in Chapter 5).
- Scan current journals and *Psychology Today*.
- Choose a topic you are genuinely interested in. This will keep you motivated.
- Talk to your professor about your ideas to be sure you are on target.
- Select a topic that has personal meaning or importance for you.
- Consult experts on your campus who might steer you toward helpful resources.

- If everything is interesting to you and you can't make up your mind, flip a coin. If the decision of chance is not acceptable, then you really do have a preference.

- Don't select a topic that is too broad or complex.

- Stay away from topics you know other students are exploring. This will keep you from competing for library materials and grades.

- Consider writing on a topic that pertains to your career aspirations.

- If your topic selection is not working for you, choose another. Choice of a topic does not always come in an inspired moment. It is often a process.

- Talk with a reference librarian.

CHAPTER 5

USING THE
LIBRARY

ACCORDING to the *Guinness Book of Records*, the largest library in the world is the Library of Congress in Washington, DC. Founded in 1800, it has accumulated over 100 million items (the typical college library holds about 200,000 volumes). The entire building has over 64 acres of floor space and more than 530 miles of bookshelves. It holds some of the world's most valuable books. The first book ever printed with movable type, the Gutenberg Bible, was purchased by the Library of Congress for $400,000.

Libraries are amazing and enthralling places. Unfortunately, I have found that many students have received little formal training on how to use a library effectively. Students typically have had a superficial exposure to the catalog and sometimes a periodical index. For too many students, their campus library remains a labyrinth of endless shelves, confusing codes, and mysterious directories.

Often the statement "There's nothing on my topic in the library" results from a student's inability to locate available material. This chapter is about the bibliographic tools that can help you find what it takes to write successful psychology papers. If you have not explored your college library, familiarize yourself with the floor plan. The information desk may have a fact sheet that will help you form a mental map of the library's various sections. There may also be scheduled tours of the library throughout the year, and at some colleges the library offers a credit course on how to find and use information (Reed & Baxter, 1983).

REFERENCE LIBRARIANS

The best resource in libraries is not a computer terminal or a book. It's the people who work there. Reference librarians, usually located in a central reference room, are trained explorers. They can guide you through a jungle of information; all you have to do is ask.

Conscientious reference librarians will be glad to assist you with your writing project. Their specialty is information retrieval and they know how to search for information in many ways and in many places. So don't be afraid to ask for guidance. Librarians derive personal and professional satisfaction from helping you find what you need.

When asking for help, however, it is important to give the librarian a complete picture of your project. This allows the librarian to show you what you need rather than what you think you need. It is also important to begin the search process early to allow yourself and the librarian plenty of time. I have often found that a librarian will discover a valuable resource for me a few days after our initial contact. Don't expect much if you are pressuring a librarian to help you because your paper is due tomorrow.

THE CATALOG

One of the easiest ways to search for what is available in the library is by using the catalog. Traditionally this has been called the card catalog. However, many college libraries now provide a computerized version that contains the same information as found on the cards.

The traditional card catalog consists of thousands of 3 x 5-inch index cards that appear in alphabetical order in dozens of file drawers. There are usually three types of catalog cards: (1) author cards, (2) title cards, and (3) subject cards. These cards are arranged alphabetically in the drawers. Some libraries have a separate card catalog for subject cards, while other simply file all the cards together.

Many libraries have a computerized catalog that can save you time. Such online systems are automated and user friendly. While some libraries rely entirely on a computerized system, others use a card catalog for older books and a computer system for more recent acquisitions. In either case, you will want to familiarize yourself with the on-line catalog.

Libraries use different types of computerized catalogs, but the search process is similar for each system. You will be required to enter information into the computer and it will lead you to the sources you desire. On-line systems allow you to search by author, title, and subject just as you would with the card catalog. Some systems may also allow you to search by keyword, year of publication, or even by call number. Once you locate the desired information, the system will allow you to print the results of your search.

There are other types of catalogs. Your college library may use a microform catalog system which uses microfilm on long reels of film or microfiche (pronounced micro-fish), which are 4 x 6-inch clear plastic cards. These catalogs contain the same information as found in the card catalog but take up much less space within the library building. Microfilm or microfiche systems work on machines that allow you to scan for items of interest.

Regardless of the catalog system your library uses, you will need to be able to locate the *call number* (a sequence of letters and numbers specified by the Library of Congress). On cards, this number is located in the upper-left corner (cards also contain other technical information useful to librarians. See Exhibit 1). With on-line catalogs, the call number is prominently displayed on the screen. A book's call number indicates exactly where the book is stored in the library stacks. The stacks are coded according to categories that coincide with the numbers and letters on the index card. A book's call number will appear at the bottom of its spine.

Exhibit 1 Sample Author Catalog Card

```
616.8914      Lazarus, Arnold A
L431p                 The practice of multimodal therapy:  systematic,
           comprehensive, and effective psychotherapy /
Arnold A. Lazarus. — New York:  McGraw-Hill,
c1981.

                      x, 272 p. : ill. ; 24 cm.


                      Bibliography: pp. 245—255
                      Included indexes.
                      ISBN  0-07-03813-9


                      1. Psychotherapy. 2. Title.
                      [DNLM: 1.  Psychotherapy.  WM420 L431p]


           RC480.L39       616.89'14        80-29561


           Library of Congress
```

GENERAL PSYCHOLOGICAL REFERENCE MATERIAL

Every library has a reference section. It contains resources such as almanacs, dictionaries, and encyclopedias. Beyond general encyclopedias such as *World Book* and *Britannica,* your library will probably have specialized reference books related specifically to psychology. Here are a few examples:

Benner, D. G. (Ed.) (1985). *Baker encyclopedia of psychology.* Grand Rapids, MI: Baker Book House.

Corsini, R. J. (Ed.) (1994). *Encyclopedia of psychology* (4 vols.). New York: Wiley.

Eysenck, J. J., Arnold, W., & Meili, R. (Eds.) (1972). *Encyclopedia of psychology* (3 vols.). London: Search Press.

Goldenson, R. M. (1970). *The encyclopedia of human behavior: Psychology, psychiatry, and mental health* (Vols. 1 & 2). Garden City, NY: Doubleday.

Gregory, R. L. (Ed.) (1987). *The Oxford companion to the mind.* New York: Oxford University Press.

Harre, R., & Lamb, R. (Eds.) (1983). *The encyclopedic dictionary of psychology.* Cambridge, MA: MIT Press.

Wolman, B. B. (Ed.) (1977-1983). *International encyclopedia of psychiatry, psychology, psychoanalysis, and neurology* (Vols. 1-12). New York: Van Nostrand Reinhold.

The *Subject Guide to Books in Print* is an annual publication that lists all English language, in-print, and forthcoming nonfiction titles from nearly 14,000 publishers. In companion volumes, publications are listed by their authors and titles. This guide is useful when trying to locate current books on a specific topic. To locate older books on a topic, consult the *Cumulative Book Index.*

INDEXES AND ABSTRACTS RELATED TO PSYCHOLOGY

Most published psychological research appears in the form of journal articles. (See the Appendix for a listing of journals related to psychology.) The library's catalog, however, does not usually index specific articles within journals. The primary index for locating these articles is *Psychological Abstracts,* an indexing-abstracting service of psychological literature covering English language journals, monographs, proceedings, dissertations, reports, and conference papers. The indexed items contain complete bibliographic information and a brief summary of the item's content. The database service is updated monthly by the American

Psychological Association. *Psychological Abstracts* is the most important index of psychological research. We'll talk about using this service in the next chapter.

Besides the printed format of *Psychological Abstracts*, it is also available in a computer format — either the on-line version or the compact-disc (CD-ROM) version. The on-line system is called PsycINFO, and the compact-disc system is called PsycLIT (it is updated quarterly). The next chapter describes how to use these computer formats.

There are other indexing and abstracting services of interest to students of psychology. They include the following:

- *The Educational Resources Information Center* (ERIC) covers a broad range of interests and many types of research. It is a clearinghouse for research on educational psychology, testing, counseling, child development, evaluation research, and so on. ERIC indexes journal articles as well as an extensive collection of unpublished materials, such as papers, presentations, and theses which are available on microfiche in many college libraries.

- *Sociological Abstracts* provides brief summaries of journals from around the world in sociology and related disciplines.

- *Social Work Research and Abstracts* is a journal which also provides brief summaries of journals pertaining to social work and counseling.

- *Social Sciences Index* includes the major psychology and other social science journals which are in the collections of most college or university libraries.

- *Social Science Citation Index* is an international multidisciplinary index to the literature of the social, behavioral, and related sciences.

- *Dissertation Abstracts International* is a monthly series of abstracts of doctoral dissertations from more than 400 universities in the United States and Canada. It is published in three volumes, one for the humanities and social sciences, another for the natural sciences, and a third for international dissertations. Selected dissertation abstracts are also indexed in *Psychological Abstracts*.

- *Reader's Guide to Periodical Literature* is a subject index of articles published in major popular magazines such as *Time, Saturday Review, Scientific American, Evening Post, Psychology Today, Sports Illustrated*, and so on. While these resources are considered "popular" and not scholarly, and while their coverage of the behavioral sciences is not comprehensive, they can be helpful secondary sources in establishing content and a rationale for a paper. The *Reader's Guide to Periodical Literature* is available in computerized format in some libraries.

- *InfoTrac* and *Academic Abstract* are other services that also offer computerized access to mostly popular and some scholarly articles. Ask a reference librarian which system your library has and how it works.

EVERYTHING YOU COULD ASK FOR

Thanks to the service of interlibrary loan (ILL), most libraries can obtain nearly any book or article you need — even if it is something your library does not own in its collection. The smallest of libraries has access to millions of books and journals on any subject you can imagine. If your library does not have a particular book or journal on one of its shelves, you can request that they borrow it from another library. This service is inexpensive and sometimes free. However, it will take a few days to process your requests, so plan your ILL usage in advance (Reed & Baxter, 1983).

USING THE INTERNET WITHOUT WASTING YOUR TIME

IF you are one of the 30 million cybernauts now on-line, you are probably already aware of how useful the Internet can be in finding psychological information. You are probably also aware of how time consuming surfing the Net can become if you don't know how and where to find what you are looking for. On the other hand, if you are among the few remaining millions who have not surfed the Web, you will want to learn how to use this easily accessible, inexpensive, and valuable research tool.

Despite commercialization, the Internet could be described as the world's largest library. Its bibliographies, abstracts, full-text journal articles, lectures, and research projects are merely a "mouse click" away from your desktop. New Web sites are being added every day and access to authoritative information on specialized topics is current, convenient, and seemingly limitless (Chapter 18 will show you how to reference this information according to APA style). If you are thinking that the Internet is going to have everything you need to write your psychology paper, however, think again. The Net can serve you well, but it is most often a means to augment the more traditional library work most psychology papers require.

WHAT IS THE INTERNET?

The idea for the Internet began in the late 1960s when scientists at four universities (Stanford, UCLA, University of California at Santa Barbara, and University of Utah) wanted to use their computers to communicate with each other in a quick and economical fashion. Eventually, U.S. military sites were added to the network of computers and services included electronic mail (e-mail). By the 1980s, the National Science Foundation developed its own network of supercomputers around the country and funded the remote access of educational, government, and global research facilities. This connected about 200 host computers — and the Internet was born.

In recent years, the government has collaborated with private industry to build the "information superhighway" with an estimated 9 million hosts. It is estimated that by the year 2000 there will be more than 100 million Internet service providers.

You connect to the Internet by dialing another computer though your modem (a telephone hook-up to your personal computer). Currently, there are three basic types of access to the Internet: a gateway or dedicated connection though a school or office, a direct or dial-up service provider, or an on-line indirect service provider. Some fortunate students may have free access to the Internet through a university that has a gateway connection.

WHAT DOES THE INTERNET DO?

Once connected to the Internet, the most popular way to access information is through the World Wide Web. The web contains documents (or pages) from around the world and is the most comprehensive, user-friendly interface. The documents on the web are written in Hypertext — a command language that allows a "link" to another web page instantly, taking you to another site rather than just giving a reference. For instance, if you are reading a biographical sketch of a psychology professor at a university, links within the text may send you to the university's home page, the professor's latest articles, or a link to a colleague's page on multicultural counseling — all contained in one document.

Each page on the Web has an address, or URL (Uniform Resource Locator). The URL contains the location of the document you want to retrieve, which may be a file on a computer down the street or an Internet site halfway around the world. The Web has millions of addresses and keeping track of where you have been and where you might like to return is done by "bookmarking" sites along the way

In addition to remaining an educational and scientific resource, the Internet's ever-evolving conveniences include the ability to check weather conditions, order flowers, make on-line travel arrangements, purchase catalog items, find specific addresses, and explore investment decisions. The possibilities are virtually endless. You can even order a birthday card to be sent to a friend's e-mail address. Oh, and you can research topics and issues in psychology. Truthfully, the services are too many to mention. Although these services are all available on the Internet, your access to them may be limited by the service provider you select. It is important to determine your needs before getting connected.

GETTING WHERE YOU WANT TO GO

A toolkit of sorts, known as a "search engine" is what one uses to research topics on the Internet. It allows you to enter a word or phrase to identify what you are interested in and it will return all the web sites that contain that word or phrase. If your search term is something very common, like "psychology," the search becomes fruitless because that word appears on several hundred-thousand web sites. For this reason, each search engine has information on how to narrow your search to a specific subject.

Some of the most common search tools include the following:

Alta Vista	http://altavista.digital.com
Excite	http://www.excite.com
Lycos	http://www.lycos.com
Open Text Index	http://www.opentext.com
Yahoo	http://www.yahoo.com

While each of these search tools organize the web by broad subjects (such as education, mental health, travel and sports), you will still have to spend time narrowing your search to fit your needs.

Library and commercial databases also are available on the Internet for retrieving bibliographies and abstracts. ERIC (Educational Resources Information Center) is available on-line (http://ericir.syr.edu) and so are the catalogues of many universities around the world. Commercial databases usually offer free bibliography searches but charge for sending you the actual article. UNCOVER (http://www.carl.org/carlweb) is a comprehensive database offering one hour delivery on many journal articles, via fax or e-mail. NlightN (http://www.nlightn.com) is another on-line service provided by The Library Corporation.   Its database includes the American Psychological Association's PsycINFO and the subset PsycLIT.

PSYCHOLOGY ON THE INTERNET

The following search tools will be of particular relevance to the study of psychology:

American Counseling Association	http://www.counseling.org
American Psychological Association	http://www.apa.org
Behavior OnLine	http://www.behavior.net
American Association of Marriage and Family Therapists	http://www.aamft.org

To learn how to use the Internet more efficiently in tracking down relevant material, see D. Kelley-Milburn and M. A. Milburn's article "Cyberspace: Resources for Psychologists on the Internet," which appeared in *Psychological Science* (1995), Vol. 6, pp. 203–11.

CHAPTER 7

PREPARING A WORKING REFERENCE LIST

THE most impressive foundation for a building I have ever heard of is found in India. It was laid in 1290 by the Rajah of Bedar. In a dream, he was advised to build a fortress on golden underpinnings. When he awoke, he followed through. His craftsmen excavated the earth while he had the royal treasury emptied of 50,000 gold bricks totaling 37,500 pounds. The gold was lowered into the ground to form a 14-karat foundation that remains to this day. That gold is worth over $16,000,000 in today's market.

I'm not sure how one could justify a solid-gold foundation, but no one would argue that a building's foundation is its most important component. Without a solid foundation, a house would never stand. Building a psychology paper's reference list is like pouring a foundation. If you work at establishing a good reference list, the rest of your paper will be much easier to construct.

There are two modes of searching the literature to collect information that can become your working reference list. The first mode is to search by hand. This means taking notes on bibliographic sources by using *Psychological Abstracts* (mentioned in the previous chapter and below). The second mode is accessing information through a computer. Many projects will involve a combination of these two modes.

USING *PSYCHOLOGICAL ABSTRACTS*, PSYCINFO, AND PSYCLIT

Lynn Cameron and James Hart (1992) have studied the differences between students who understand and use library research strategies, especially electronic information retrieval methods, and found that students who have mastered PsycLIT, for example, experience less anxiety and are more confident than those who have not. Other researchers have found that students are "overwhelmingly pleased" with these methods (Schultz and Salomon, 1990, p. 56). For these reasons, not to mention your GPA and how much you learn, it will be worth your while to master the psychology research tool available in your campus library, whether it be *Psychological Abstracts*, PsycINFO, or PsycLIT.

These resources will allow you to conduct speedy searches through massive amounts of literature. By using them you can locate specific articles and books that will help you write your paper. And you can search through years of manuscripts in just minutes to read brief reviews (abstracts) of potentially helpful manuscripts. *Psychological Abstracts* covers the period from 1927 to the present. PsycINFO covers 1967 to the present and PsycLIT covers 1974 to the present. Both PsycINFO and PsycLIT cover books from 1987 to the present. Exhibit 2 summarizes the comparisons of *Psychological Abstracts*, PsycINFO, and PsycLIT.

Exhibit 2 Comparing *Psychological Abstracts*, PsycINFO, & PsycLIT

	Psychological Abstracts	**PsycINFO**	**PsycLIT**
Format	print	on-line	CD-ROM
Coverage	journals, technical reports, and books	journals, books, and technical reports (including non-English)	journals and books (including non-English)
Dates	1927 to present, books: 1992 to present	1967 to present, books: 1987 to present	1974 to present, books: 1987 to present
Updates	monthly	monthly	quarterly

To use *Psychological Abstracts* you will first need to select proper search terms that will help you pare down the search and retrieve only the most useful information. For this, the American Psychological Association's *Thesaurus of Psychological Index Terms* (1991) is invaluable. It is usually located in the reference section of your library. This thesaurus is based on the vocabulary used in psychology and related disciplines and it will tell you what terms will locate your desired articles. It can save you a lot of time and effort. For example, if you are searching for articles on "depression," you may neglect several important terms that can help you pinpoint more precisely what you are looking for.   Exhibit 3 is an example from the *Thesaurus of Psychological Index Terms*:

Exhibit 3   Sample from *Thesaurus of Psychological Index Terms**

SAMPLE   EXPLANATION

Major Depression [88]   *Index term*
PN 4162   **SC** 29143   *Posting note and subject code*
SN Affective disorder marked by dysphoric   *Scope note*
mood, inactivity, and self deprecation.
Consider DEPRESSION (EMOTION)
to access references prior to 1988.
UF Agitated Depression   *Used for term*
     Dysphoria
     Melancholia
     Psychotic Depressive Reaction
     Unipolar Depression
B   Affective Disturbances   *Broader term*
N   Anaclitic Depression   *Narrower terms*
     Dysthymic Disorder
     Endogenous Depression
     Involutional Depression
     Neurotic Depressive Reaction
     Postpartum Depression
     Reactive Depression
R   Depression (Emotion)   *Related terms*
     Manic Depression
     Mental Disorders

Once you have made a list of appropriate thesaurus terms for your search, go to the "Brief Subject Index" located in the back of each issue of *Psychological Abstracts* (for older issues you may use the annual Subject Index, which has indexing for an entire year).   In the subject index, locate the terms you selected from the thesaurus.   Following each of these terms you will see a string of numbers.   These numbers refer to the main entry section of *Psychological Abstracts*.   All you need to do is match the numbers to the entries to find a citation and abstract from an article on your topic.   You can then read the abstract to see if the item is appropriate.   Remember, if your library doesn't have the article you locate, you may use interlibrary loan, as discussed in Chapter 5.

*Reprinted with permission of the American Psychological Association.

Most libraries with PsycINFO (the on-line system) have a librarian that will perform the search with you. Before you begin your search, talk with the librarian about choosing key words and descriptors from the *Thesaurus*. This will help you retrieve only the most useful information and it will save you money if there is a fee for the search.

Many college libraries provide PsycLIT (the CD-ROM system) for students to use at no charge. You can quickly learn how to maneuver around in PsycLIT by using its on-screen tutorial. Some libraries have a tutorial video to help you as well. In any case, you will quickly see that the PsycLIT system is user-friendly and also timesaving. PsycLIT does not have a lot of complicated commands to memorize. The computer will give you a "menu" or list of selections at the bottom of the screen and all you have to do is respond to the prompts the system gives you. If you are unsure how to proceed or have questions, ask a reference librarian for assistance. Your library may also have the following printed guides explaining the system: *PsycLIT Quick Reference Guide* (1992); *PsycLIT Quick Reference Guide* (1992); and *Searching PsycLIT on CD-ROM* (n.d.).

As with the other types of searches, you will want to consult the *Thesaurus of Psychological Index Terms* to select appropriate search terms for PsycLIT. However, unlike the printed paper index, PsycLIT allows you to combine these terms in a variety of ways by using what is called "Boolean logic." You may be familiar with this from studying "Venn diagrams" or "Set Theory." Basically it comes down to using three simple words, "or," "and," and "not." By using these three words and the terms from the *Thesaurus*, you will be able to search the database easily and efficiently.

When you use "or," you are telling the computer you want records containing either term. For example, you might search for "rewards" OR "incentives." Using the term "or" increases the number of citations in your search.

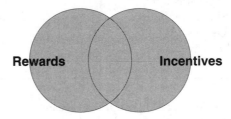

When you use "and," you are telling the computer you want records containing both terms. For example, both "rewards" AND "incentives." This will give you fewer results.

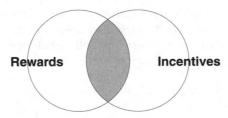

When you use "not," you are telling the computer you want records that do not contain a certain term. For example, "rewards" NOT "incentives." "Not" is a powerful operator and should be used sparingly. It may eliminate records you would rather keep.

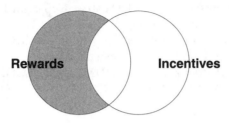

You may combine terms and operators in any number of combinations to expand or limit your search results. You'll want to keep in mind that PsycLIT is an international database and includes a number of articles which are not in English. If you want to limit your search to English only, you will type LA=English and combine that set with an "and" to your other criteria. As you become more proficient with PsycLIT you can create even more complex searches. To learn more about advanced searching methods, see the guides mentioned above or ask a reference librarian. A live demonstration by a librarian can be very beneficial (Bostain and Robbins, 1990).

Records generated by a computer search with PsycINFO or PsycLIT will contain several pieces of information, or fields, some parts of it more useful than others. See Exhibit 4.

Exhibit 4 Sample Record from PsycLIT*

TI: Morning and night couples: The effect of wake and sleep patterns on marital adjustment.
AU: Larson,-Jeffry-H.; Crane,-D.-Russell; Smith,-Craig-W.
IN: Brigham Young U, Counseling & Development Ctr, Provo, UT, US
JN: Journal-of-Marital-and-Family-Therapy; 1991 Jan Vol 17(1) 53-65
IS: 0914472X
LA: English
PY: 1991
AB: Explored the effects of spouses' wake and sleep patterns (WSPs) on marital adjustment in 150 couples who completed questions on WSPs, marital interaction, marital adjustment, and problem solving. Couples whose WSPs were mismatched (e.g., an evening person married to a morning person) reported significantly less marital adjustment, more marital conflict, less time spent in serious conversation, less time spent in shared activities, and less frequent sexual intercourse than matched couples. Contrary to expecta-

---

* Reprinted with permission of the American Psychological Association.

tions, matched night couples did not report more involvement in extrafamil-ial social activities than morning couples. Mismatched couples with high marital adjustment reported more flexibility and adaptability in their marital problem solving. Implications of these findings for premarital and marital counseling are discussed. (PsycLIT Database Copyright 1992 American Psy-chological Assn, all rights reserved)

KP: matching of spouses' wake & sleep circadian rhythms; marital adjust-ment & interaction & conflict resolution; couples

DE: MARITAL-RELATIONS; HUMAN-BIOLOGICAL-RHYTHMS; SLEEP-WAKE-CYCLE; MARITAL-CONFLICT; SPOUSES-; ADULT-HOOD-

CC: 2950; 29

PO: Human

AG: Adult

UD: 9203

AN: 79-08899

JC: 1940

The following is what the coding for the fields on the left side of the record stands for. Of course, the most meaningful information to you will probably be the TI (title), AU (author(s)), JN (journal), PY (publication year), and the AB (ab-stract). In addition, you should be aware of the DE (descriptors) and KP (key phrases) because you might want to use them in your next search. Here is the to-tal list of coded information in the record (just to satisfy your curiosity):

TI: Title
AU: Author(s)
IN: Institution
JN: Journal
IS: International Standard Serial Number
LA: Language
PY: Publication Year
AB: Abstract
KP: Key Phrases
DE: Descriptors
CC: Content Classification Code
PO: Population
AG: Age
UD: Update (when record was added to the database)
AN: Accession Number
JC: Journal Code

The coding is similar when searching for books:

AG: Composite Age Group(s)
AN: Accession Number
AT: Audience Type Code
AU: Author
AX: Auxiliary Materials
BK: Parent Book Information (chapter records only)
CA: Corporate Author(s)
CC: Classification Code(s)
CF: Conference Information
CH: Selected Chapters
CR: Content Representation
DE: Descriptors
DN: Descriptive Note
DT: Document Type Code
IN: Institutional Affiliation of First Author
IS: International Standard Book Number
LA: Language
PB: Publication Information
PO: Population
PY: Publication Year
RF: References
RN: Reprint Note
SE: Series Title
SP: Institutional Sponsors
TC: Table of Contents
TI: Book Title or Chapter Title
UD: Update Code

HANDBOOKS

Another excellent source for preparing a working reference list is handbooks. They provide succinct summaries of a particular area and are written by experts in the field. Handbooks are more comprehensive than most textbooks and provide many relevant references that will help you get started on establishing a reference list to work from (Stock, 1985).

The following list of handbooks is certainly not exhaustive and since some fields change rapidly, there may be more recent editions available.

Borgatta, E. F., & Lamberg, W. W. (Eds.). (1968). *Handbook of personality theory and research*. Chicago: Rand McNally.

Dunnette, M. D. (Ed.). (1979). *Handbook of industrial and organizational psychology*. Chicago: Rand McNally.

Gambrill, E. D. (1977). *Behavior modification: A handbook of assessment, intervention and evaluation*. San Francisco: Jossey-Bass.

Kling, J. W., et al. (1971). *Woodworth and Schlossberg's experimental psychology* (3rd ed.). New York: Holt, Rinehart and Winston.

Knutson, J. N. (Ed.). (1973). *Handbook of political psychology*. San Francisco: Jossey-Bass.

Mussen, P. H. (Ed.). (1983). *Carmichael's manual of child psychology* (4th ed.). New York: Wiley.

Struening, E. L., & Guttentag, M. (Eds.). (1975). *Handbook of evaluation research*. Beverly Hills, CA: Sage.

University of Nebraska, Department of Psychology. (1953—present). *Current theory and research in motivation, a symposium*. (Vols. 1+). Lincoln: University of Nebraska Press.

Wolman, B. B. (Ed.). (1973). *Handbook of general psychology*. Englewood Cliffs, NJ: Prentice-Hall.

Woody, R. H. (Ed.). (1980). *Encyclopedia of clinical assessment*. San Francisco: Jossey-Bass.

DOS AND DON'TS OF ESTABLISHING A REFERENCE LIST

- Before beginning your literature search, ask your professor to recommend key works that should be consulted.
- Follow up on references from psychology textbooks.
- References in specialized encyclopedias and handbooks can help you form the beginnings of a reference list.
- Realize that finding useful resources can take time. You will become unnecessarily anxious if you expect to complete your search in one sitting.
- Be patient. By giving yourself ample time to do a thorough job, you will feel more confident and understand your topic more thoroughly.
- Focus on quality rather than quantity. Superficial resources will detract from the time you could spend on more important sources.
- When your library does not have a specific work you want, use interlibrary loan.
- Remember library etiquette: Work quietly, never write in library books or journals, do not monopolize material, and please do not steal or tear out pages.
- Ask a reference librarian for assistance.

CHAPTER 8

OUTLINING THE PAPER

WHEN we lived in Pasadena, California, our home was just blocks from the prestigious California Institute of Technology. It is an impressive school. I would often marvel at the brilliant scholars consumed in their scientific studies. Its faculty is known worldwide. Even Albert Einstein taught at Cal-Tech.

In 1933 Einstein was visiting Dr. Geno Gutenberg, Cal-Tech's senior seismologist, and discussing the science of earthquakes. Einstein was asking questions as they strolled around the campus. Suddenly an excited professor broke in on their conversation. They looked around to see people rushing from nearby buildings — and to see the earth quaking under their feet! Gutenberg later confessed they had become so involved in talking about the science of earth movements they failed to notice the famous Los Angeles earthquake taking place around them.

It's difficult to imagine how we can become so focused on details that we fail to see the big picture. Psychologists call the big picture a gestalt, a wholistic completion. To ensure that you are continually reminded of the big picture while writing a paper, you need a good outline.

Writing a paper without an outline would be like traveling cross-country without a map. An outline shows you the logical progression of significant points. It keeps you from going off on tangents and helps you develop ideas that are integrally related to your topic. It also keeps you from leaving out important elements.

GETTING ORGANIZED

It should be kept in mind that an outline is often modified as you go along and get new information and ideas for organizing your paper. Your initial outline is sometimes called a *scratch outline*. It is simply a list of points to be covered that give you direction as you write. Eventually, the scratch outline will become more formal as it reflects a structure that is carefully thought out.

If you dread the idea of outlining a paper, you're not alone. Many associate the task with a junior high school English class. Back then it was hard and tedious work. Worst of all, it was graded! Relax. The outline you build for your paper is just for you. It will make your assignment easier.

To begin an outline, consider the big issues, the themes related to your topic. You can do this by grouping the information you have accumulated from your library search under several general headings. These will become the main divisions in your paper. Within these general divisions you can place related ideas and facts (along with their references). You might find it helpful to write your outline in whole sentences first (Howard & Barton, 1986).

Each major division is typically noted as a roman numeral and each of the subheadings follow in descending order. See Exhibit 5.

Exhibit 5 Illustration of Outline Progression

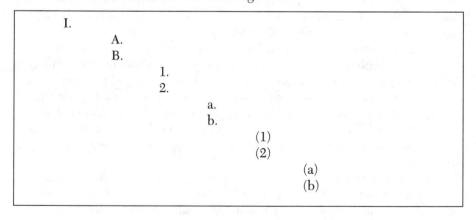

There should usually be two or more subtopics under any topic. In other words, if you list I, you should list II, and so on. If you only had one roman numeral, that point would simply be your overall paper topic.

With a clearly organized outline, your paper will almost write itself. But how do you know if your outline is clearly organized? The key is to be sure that your ideas build on one another; that there are points supporting each of the main ideas; and that the main ideas are equally developed.

If you are writing an experimental report on a study you conducted, rather than a term paper reviewing other studies, your outline is preestablished. The structure involves eight parts (APA, 1994): (1) title page, (2) abstract, (3) introduction, (4) method, (5) results, (6) discussion, (7) references, and (8) appendix. This skeleton is simply waiting to be fleshed out. These components will be described in Part Three.

WRITING THE FIRST DRAFT

CESAR RITZ was a perfectionist. A few hours before the gala opening of his famous Ritz Hotel in Paris in 1898, he came into the dining room to check on the final preparations. Ritz sat down at a table and noticed at once it was about two centimeters too high. He sat at another table. It was two centimeters too high. So were a third and a fourth table. Ritz gave a few orders and by eight o'clock the legs of all tables in the dining room had been shortened.

Cesar Ritz's son Charles, remembers that his father tried out every new mattress he ordered by sleeping one night on it. If he didn't sleep well, the mattress was returned.

As admirable as this quality might be, it would do little for Ritz if he were writing the first draft of a psychology paper. Perfectionism is not the goal of a first draft. Once you've developed an outline, your task is to support each of your points — simply as a draft. And that's a relief. You don't have to expect too much from a first draft.

The goal of your first draft is nothing more than getting your initial ideas down on paper. This may mean you don't start with the first sentence of the paper or even your introduction. Begin with a section that flows easily. You can come back to other sections later. And forget perfection! It will only cause you to stare at a blank sheet of paper or a blinking cursor on a blank computer screen for hours. John Steinbeck gave some excellent advice for getting started: "Write freely and as rapidly as possible and throw the whole thing on paper. Never correct or rewrite until the whole thing is down. Rewriting in progress is usually found to be an excuse for not going on." Don't worry about spelling, punctuation, or grammar at this stage. Your only concern is to get your ideas on paper (Hubbuch, 1985).

FIRST DRAFT WRITING TIPS

- Double- or triple-space your first draft to allow you plenty of room for future revisions. Of course this is not necessary if you are using a word processor.
- Always number your pages as you are writing. This will help you avoid later confusion.
- Write on only one side of each piece of paper.
- NOTE COMPLETE REFERENCE INFORMATION AS YOU WORK. As you quote or paraphrase another writer, cite the reference immediately.
- If a paragraph does not seem to be coming out right, refer back to your outline. Ask yourself, "What is the point I want to make here?"
- Keep your professor's grading criteria in mind. Are your arguments valid? Are they consistent? Are your conclusions realistic? Are your points important and your explanations clear?
- *Just do it!*

AVOIDING PLAGIARISM

SEVERAL years ago a friend invited me to a chapel service at West Point Military Academy. During this particular service the cadets said a prayer that I found very meaningful. My friend, knowing that I liked it, later sent me a printed copy. This is what it said: "Make us choose the harder right instead of the easier wrong, and never to be contented with half truth when whole truth can be won. Endow us with courage that is born of loyalty to all that is noble and worthy, that scores to compromise with vice and injustice and knows no fear when right and truth are in jeopardy."

This prayer is repeated every Sunday in chapel services at West Point. And it's not a bad prayer for any student at any school — especially when it comes to writing papers. The temptation is often present for students to take "the easier wrong" in writing assignments by turning to plagiarism. Taking "the harder right," however, forgoes this deceitful practice for students of noble character.

WHAT IS PLAGIARISM?

Plagiarism strikes fear into any student who understands its sobering consequences: being flunked, being placed on disciplinary probation, or even being expelled from school. Plagiarism is serious. It occurs when a student copies statements from another source and presents them to the instructor without giving credit to the real author (Walter & Siebert, 1990). Sometimes it occurs on purpose. Sometimes it's unintentional. In either case it's not acceptable.

The term "plagiarize" comes from the Latin word *plagium* meaning "to kidnap." And in a very real sense, the student who plagiarizes is a kidnapper, a literary thief.

"I borrow from other writers shamelessly," wrote Thornton Wilder. "I can only say in my defense, like the woman brought before the judge on a charge of kleptomania, 'I do steal; but, Your Honor, only from the very best stores.'" There is nothing wrong with "stealing" from other authors — as long as you give them credit. There are two kinds of plagiarism. *Direct plagiarism* is quoting word for word the work of another and not giving credit. *Indirect plagiarism* comes from paraphrasing another's writing without giving credit to the original author for the ideas. In either case you can avoid it simply by using quotation marks and/or noting your sources (Walvoord, 1982).

LEARNING BY EXAMPLE

Consider the following section from a student's paper:

> The evidence for adverse medical effects from anger, anxiety, and depression is overwhelming. Both anger and anxiety can make people more prone to a wide range of diseases. And while depression may not make people more vulnerable to becoming ill, it does seem to slow down medical recovery, especially for patients with severe conditions.

Not bad, is it? Well, you might answer differently if you were Daniel Goleman. He's the author of *Emotional Intelligence* (1995) and this student's paragraph looks amazingly similar to what Goleman wrote on page 177 of his book:

> The cumulative evidence for adverse medical effects from anger, anxiety, and depression, then, is compelling. Both anger and anxiety, when chronic, can make people more susceptible to a range of disease. And while depression may not make people more vulnerable to becoming ill, it does seem to impede medical recovery and heighten the risk of death, especially with more frail patients with severe conditions.

Recognize the striking similarity? That's plagiarism! Well, how could you convey the ideas of this paragraph without plagiarizing? The answer is found in giving credit where credit is due. The following paragraph makes use of quotes and properly cites the author for his ideas:

> Goleman (1995) has determined that the evidence clearly shows adverse medical effects from anger, anxiety, and depression. He has found that chronic anger and anxiety "can make people more prone to a wide range of diseases" (p. 177).

```
Patients with severe conditions of depression, according to
Goleman, do not recover from their medical conditions as
well as those patients who do not suffer from depression.
```

Do you see the difference? It is perfectly acceptable to report someone else's ideas and findings as long as you give them credit by name and by page number if you are quoting them directly (see Chapter 18 for more specific information on how to reference quotes). By the way, don't think that you can steer clear of plagiarism by simply saturating your paper with quotation marks. Rarely should you quote long passages in your paper. After all, the purpose of the paper is for you to work at finding, conceptualizing, and synthesizing your own thoughts by learning from others. If you are simply quoting other writers again and again, it will be obvious that you do not understand the material well enough to write about it yourself.

I once had a mathematics professor who, before giving a test, would say something like this: "I'm giving you two examinations today. One in statistics and the other in honesty. I hope you will pass them both. If you must fail one, fail statistics. There are many good people in the world who can pass stats, but there are no good people in the world who cannot pass the examination of honesty." I echo my former professor's admonishment to you when it comes to plagiarism in writing psychology papers.

CHAPTER 11

REWRITING AND THE FINAL DRAFT

MICHELANGELO was one of the greatest sculptors of all time. His masterpieces include *La Pietà, Madonna of Bruges, Moses,* and *Madonna and Child.* Michelangelo could find beauty in stone that other artists would never touch. Agostiono d'Antonio, a sculptor from Florence, Italy, worked diligently but unsuccessfully on a large piece of marble. He finally gave up. Other sculptors, too, worked with the piece of marble, but they also gave up. The stone was discarded. It lay on a rubbish heap for 40 years. Michelangelo, out strolling one day, saw the stone and had it brought to his studio. From that seemingly worthless stone, he carved one of the world's masterpieces — *David*!

Writing is a lot like sculpting. Your first draft demands chiseling deep cuts into the marble to form a vague structure. Its roughness seems to reveal nothing that could be of value. But just as Michelangelo delicately worked stone, an effective writer rewrites again and again to sculpt a masterful paper.

Experienced and effective writers revise their work many times. Words rarely arrive on a page as a finished product. Revising helps you refine your thinking. It helps you organize a clean and tight presentation of your thoughts.

REWRITING TIPS

Don't be afraid to cut and paste. It is during this stage of writing that a word processor really pays off. It allows you to move blocks of text around with ease. If you are working with pen and paper, however, a pair of scissors and plenty of invisible tape work just fine. If a paragraph or section fits better elsewhere, simply cut and tape.

Read your draft version aloud. This is an excellent way to detect grammatical errors and unclear thinking. If you are brave, you may wish to read it aloud to another student or friend.

Before turning your paper in, have another person read it. Some instructors may even be willing to read your draft before you submit the final paper. If the instructor is not open to reading it clear through, she or he may be willing to take a quick look at it and offer an initial evaluation. In addition to boosting your grade, this will improve your writing for future assignments.

Trim the fat by eliminating or tightening your words. The Gettysburg Address required only 268 words; The Ten Commandments, 297 words; the Declaration of Independence, 300 words (a typical double-spaced page is about 300 words). Get the point? Much can be said with few words. Students often use too many prepositions. Qualifiers are also overused. E. B. White (1979) labels them as "leeches that infest the pond of prose, sucking the blood of words" (p. 73). Watch for very, quite, and really.

Avoid lengthy quotations. Long passages written by another author are usually not essential. Your paper is to be a result of your individual effort, and for the most part your own words. Long quotations convey the message that you do not understand the topic well enough to write about it yourself. On the other hand, brief quotes that are cited can add force and punch to your writing.

Allow time for your paper to get "cold." By letting it rest for at least 24 hours you can return to your completed draft with a more objective perspective. A "time out" allows you to come back to the draft refreshed and ready to judge the impact of your words more as your professor will.

Keep it simple. Some students feel they should "sound" scholarly and scientific. This is a mistake and usually results in a paper that comes out sounding complicated and obscure. A good scientist communicates ideas in simple and clear terms. Do your best to avoid jargon, big words, and long sentences. Professors will not be impressed by a complicated paper.

Double-check the paper for accuracy. Be sure you have documented each of your sources correctly.

Read the section "A Few Elements of Writing Well" (Part Four) later in this book. It will alert you to important points of grammar, punctuation, usage, spelling, and inclusive language.

Note the APA Style section later in this book. This will describe everything from margin size to where to place page numbers.

When you are ready to submit your final draft, be sure it is carefully typed and proofread for errors. Your ideas deserve the best showcase you can give them.

That includes using clean white paper (preferably bond and definitely not onion-skin or "erasable" paper) and a new typewriter ribbon or a laser printer if possible. It is also wise to bind your paper in a clean and attractive fashion (ask your professors if they have a preference).

LEARNING FROM YOUR WRITING

On a wintry day at twilight, a ragged man entered a small music shop on a side street in London. He held an old violin under his arm. He told the shop owner he was hungry and would take anything for the old instrument.

The shop owner gave him $5 and the man gratefully shuffled out into the night. When the violin's new owner drew a bow across its strings it produced a rich mellow tone. He was astonished and peered intently inside the instrument. He could not believe his eyes. He observed the name, Antonio Stradivari, and the date, 1704. It was the famous Stradivarius violin that had been missing for 100 years and was valued at more than $100,000.

The penniless man had not known the value of his possession. He lived in poverty when he could have enjoyed wealth.

Just as this man overlooked the Stradivarius, many students overlook the value in a psychology paper that has already been graded. A paper with a professor's comments on it, regardless of the grade, is worthy of study. It is a priceless source of learning. Rita Mae Brown said of those who criticized her work, "If [they] want to help me, let them come sit next to me while I'm writing." In many ways, your professors are giving you the kind of "criticism" she is referring to. Your professors are critiquing you to improve your writing, your research skills, and your thinking — not to attack you with a scathing review published the *New York Times*.

For this reason it is important to retrieve your paper once the professor has graded it. Even if it is not handed back and you submitted the paper at the end of the term and the new term has begun, it is crucial to read your professor's comments. Receiving feedback on your paper is one of the best ways to improve your writing.

For a number of reasons, some instructors don't write many comments on their students' papers. If this is the case, you may want to learn more from your instructors during their office hours. Bring your paper with you and politely explain that you want to improve your writing and would appreciate any suggestions. You can do this even if you received an A. Take notes on your professor's comments and try to implement them on your next paper.

DOS AND DON'TS

- Read each comment the professor has made.
- Ask the professor to elaborate on a comment if it is not clear to you.
- Just for practice, try rewriting the section in light of the professor's comments.
- Don't neglect your professor's positive comments about your paper. Try to replicate your strong points in future papers.
- If grammar, punctuation, or usage is a significant deterrent to improving your grade, ask one of the professors in English to look over your paper and make suggestions. He or she can give helpful advice with just a quick read. You might also consult your school's "writing lab."
- Pull out the professor's comments on your previous papers to ensure that you repeat the positives and not the mistakes.
- Remember that critical comments are designed to help you improve, not to punish you.

PART THREE

UNDERSTANDING AND USING APA STYLE

WHAT IS APA STYLE?

In the mid-1960s, former FBI director J. Edgar Hoover was reading to his top agents a typed copy of a letter that he had just dictated to his secretary. He didn't like the way she had formatted the letter, so he scribbled on the bottom "Watch the borders," and asked her to retype it. That afternoon the secretary did as she was instructed and sent the letter out. For the next two weeks FBI agents were put on special alert along the Canadian and Mexican borders.

Hoover's secretary was obviously confused! Formatting a paper, however, does not have to be the cause of misunderstanding. There are systems for documenting sources and setting margin sizes, for example, that are straightforward and easy to learn. Each of them is found in "style manuals." These manuals outline the general rules for making a paper pleasing and consistent. They answer questions such as: How wide should my margins be? Can the right margin be justified? How should I cite references? What are headings? When should I use headings? What about using charts and graphs? Style manuals also cover matters of mechanics such as punctuation, capitalization, setting up quotations, and so on.

There are two basic types of manuals: "general style manuals" and "professional style manuals." The first type includes *The Chicago Manual of Style*, and Turabian's *A Manual for Writers of Term Papers, Theses, and Dissertations*. These two books answer almost any question a professional writer could think of about proper manuscript form. For this reason, they can also be intimidating and bewildering for novices.

In addition to the general style manuals, there are style manuals developed and published by professional academic organizations such as the American Institute of Physics or the Modern Language Association.

The American Psychological Association (APA) also has a style manual called the *Publication Manual of the American Psychological Association.* APA style grows out of efforts over the past 50 years or so to define a consistent way of writing for journals published by the American Psychological Association. Because of its simplicity and clearly defined expectations, however, it is recommended by *The Chicago Manual* for all papers in the social sciences and it has been accepted as the guide for numerous disciplines.

Students in the social and behavioral sciences are often expected to follow APA style as they prepare papers. Sometimes this becomes confusing, however, because the APA *Publication Manual* (APA, 1994), now in its fourth edition, mainly addresses how to prepare reports for professional research journals, not papers for psychology courses.

This section of *How to Write Psychology Papers* will guide you in preparing effective writing assignments that are consistent with APA style. Following the principle of Occam's Razor, this section will cut to the bone and present only the essential information. If you have questions about APA style this section does not answer, please refer directly to the *Publication Manual of the American Psychological Association.* It can probably be found in your college library and bookstore. If your bookstore does not carry it, ask if they can order it.

CHAPTER 1 4

TITLE PAGE

AN ancient Chinese proverb says, "The beginning of wisdom is to call things by their right names." This is certainly true when it comes to "naming" your paper. Your paper's title provides the first impression your professor will have of your hard work, so it deserves special attention.

The title of a paper or report should summarize the main idea of your project. A good title is succinct and descriptive. One need not use unnecessary words in a title, as in "A Study of the Influence of Guilt on Empathic Concern." Simply delete the unnecessary words, "A Study of." This makes the title more compact. Robert Southey said, "It is with words as with sunbeams—the more they are condensed, the deeper they burn."

The title should stand alone and give the reader a fair idea of what the paper is all about. If the original title of a paper does not adequately describe the finished paper, change it to be more accurate and complete. A title should be succinct and rarely more than 15 words in length.

In addition to the name of the paper, the title page should contain your first and last name as the author (do not use the word *by*). You should also place the name of your college under your name. The course for which the paper was written and the professor's name should appear at the bottom of the paper, along with the date the paper was turned in. Of course, a professor may provide different requirements for a title page, but the following is a typical example:

```
                    Title of Paper
                    Student's Name
                    Name of College




                    Title of Course
                    Professor's Name
                    Date Submitted
```

For papers being submitted to a professional journal, a "running head" would also be expected to appear on the title page. A running head is an abbreviated title that is printed at the top of each page to identify each page of the manuscript. However, a running head is usually not needed for college papers.

CHAPTER 15

ABSTRACT

THE term *abstract* was first used in 1398. In Latin it means to draw away. For our purposes it means to "draw away" the essentials from the body of your paper.

The abstract is a brief summary of your paper. It gives the reader a quick, comprehensive survey of the paper's contents. An abstract should be typed as a single paragraph in block format (no paragraph indention) and appear on a single page by itself.

A typical abstract has about six sentences and it is written after the first draft of the paper is complete. In fact, once the abstract is written it can serve as a convenient guide during revisions of the paper. The structure of the paper's final version will emphasize the important points if it has stayed on track with the original abstract.

It is generally best to begin an abstract with a statement of the topic or problem addressed in the paper. For example, "Counseling adolescents is fraught with pitfalls." Or, "Repetition was tested as a training procedure for sixth graders." The remaining part of the abstract should state the paper's purpose, and the final sentence of the abstract normally states the general conclusions, implications, or applications of the research.

If you are writing an experimental paper, the abstract should also discuss the subjects, the experimental method, and the findings (including statistical significance levels). You may find it helpful to write your abstract by summarizing each major section of the paper with a single sentence. These six sentences or so, combined, will be your abstract.

The APA *Publication Manual* (1994, p. 23) describes a good abstract as being:

- *Accurate.* It should correctly reflect the contents of the paper. In other words, it should not contain information that is not in the body of the paper.

- *Self-contained.* The abstract should define all abbreviations and acronyms. For example if you are referring to "PTSD," say post-traumatic stress disorder.

- *Concise and specific.* Each sentence of the abstract should be informative and as brief as possible. Be sure each word is essential.

- *Nonevaluative.* Do not comment on what you wrote about in the paper. Simply report what the paper is about. The abstract is not a place to add your own creative insights.

- *Coherent and readable.* Write in clear prose. Don't try to impress the reader with gobbledygook and jargon.

Once you've got a polished paper, review the characteristics of a good abstract. If your abstract follows the five elements mentioned above, chances are you are on target.

CHAPTER 16

TEXT

THANKSGIVING might not be celebrated today in the United States, were it not for a persistent woman named Sarah Hale. She is better known as the author of the poem "Mary Had a Little Lamb," but her persevering vision led to a national holiday.

Thanksgiving used to be observed by a few individual states on whatever date suited their fancy. Then in 1828, Sarah Hale began campaigning for Thanksgiving as a national holiday. She wrote letters and sought appointments with national leaders including the President. Time after time she was politely rebuffed, sometimes being told it was impossible.

Finally in 1863 President Lincoln listened seriously to Ms. Hale's plea that the North and the South "lay aside enmities and strife" on a national Thanksgiving Day. Her persistence obviously paid off. Lincoln proclaimed the fourth Thursday of November to be Thanksgiving Day and we have been enjoying Ms. Hale's efforts ever since.

While writing a psychology paper may not seem as lofty as campaigning for a national holiday, it certainly requires some of the same persistence. We have explored APA style as it relates to your title page and abstract. Let's keep moving.

The body of your paper should open with an introduction that presents the topic or problem you are studying. Because the introduction is clearly identified by its position in the paper, it is not necessary that you label it as you will the other sections. Your introduction presents the paper's background. Assume that your reader has knowledge in the field and cite only research that is pertinent to the specific topic. In other words, rather than trying to cite every study ever done on your topic, select only key references. Include early classic studies to provide perspective, as well as some of the most recent research. Once you have introduced the topic or problem, justified its significance, and developed the background, you can tell what you did in the paper so the reader knows where you are headed. In brief, your introduction tells the reader what you plan to do and why you plan to do it.

If you are writing a term paper (not an experimental report) the remaining portion of your paper should be broken up with section headings that clearly note what that section is about.

PARTS OF THE EXPERIMENTAL REPORT

An experimental research paper requires formulating a research question, designing and conducting the experiment, and analyzing and interpreting the data. In an experimental research report, the outline involves the following sections:

Introduction. If your paper is experimental, your introduction should include the same qualities as a term paper (described above), and it should explain the variables and your rationale for each of your hypotheses. How do you justify the selection of your predictor variables? Provide evidence that your predictor variables have been inadequately studied in the past and are worthy of attention. If your study is a direct replication of another study, you should emphasize the importance of the original study and discuss why it is worthy of replication and what differences you expect to see.

Method. This is the "how" section of your paper. It is usually composed of four subsections: subjects, design, apparatus, and procedure. First, describe the general characteristics of the *subjects* in your study. Discuss how many there were, their ages, and how you got them to be in your study. You should also mention any other relevant characteristics and describe how the subjects were assigned to the experimental conditions. Your *design* paragraph should describe the predictor variables and the design of your study. If your study is a survey, describe all the predictor and correlated variables you measured (e.g., age, education). You should then describe the dependent variable(s) of your study. In your *apparatus* section, describe the equipment, or measures, you used. Provide enough information for your readers to be able to acquire or reproduce the materials you used. You may also wish to attach a copy of the measures in an appendix. If you used a published test, provide the name of the test and a reference. Your *procedure* section should describe, in specific terms, the differences in the instructions for experimental and control conditions. Include enough information for a reader to replicate your study. You may quote, for example, important parts of the instructions.

Results. Here you simply describe what happened in your study. Summarize your data and analyses by explaining how you obtained scores and how you analyzed the data. For example, "Ratings on the empathy scale were collected for all subjects." Or, "The ratings on the three scales were summed to give a total guilt rating." In explaining how you analyzed your data, you might write, "The differences between the scores for the two groups were analyzed by independent *t* tests." Once data are explained, you can present the important findings and how they relate to your hypothesis. Clearly state whether or not the results support your hypothesis, but don't explain the data (this will be done in the next section). Also report any statistically significant effects you did not predict.

Discussion. In this final section you should restate and explain your hypotheses. You should also summarize what your data indicated about these hypotheses and interpret your results by explaining if they are consistent with your hypotheses. Rarely do results nicely match initial hypotheses. There are almost always surprises — things you expected to find and didn't, or things you didn't expect to find and did. If you did not obtain any significant results, what kept that from happening? Discuss how you would change the study next time. Be sure to couch your discussion in the context of existing literature. Relate it to studies you reviewed in the introduction. Be sure to mention any weaknesses of your approach. Don't be embarrassed. There are no perfectly conclusive studies. Wrap up your discussion by discussing potential applications of your results as well as theoretical implications and future directions for research.

GENERAL RULES OF FORMAT

Following are the essential rules of format:

- Your paper should be typed or computer printed on one side of heavy white paper.
- Set your margins to leave 1 and 1/2 inches at the top, bottom, and both sides of each page.
- Do not justify the right margin or hyphenate words at the ends of lines. Your paper should be double-spaced throughout.
- Begin each paragraph by indenting five spaces.
- Use one space after commas and semicolons and two spaces after colons (except in ratios) and periods ending sentences.
- Number pages in the upper right-hand corner, starting with the title page. Use arabic numerals (e.g., 1, 2, 3, . . .). The only pages after the abstract that are not numbered are the figures.

CHAPTER 17

REFERENCES

THE body of your paper may be complete, but your paper is not finished until you deal with references and material to be placed in appendixes. One of the most important parts of preparing a psychology paper is properly citing references.

CITING REFERENCES

Almost any source from which you take factual information or from which you quote directly (e.g., a book, an article, or even a lecture), needs to be referenced. For example, if you adapt information from a journal article, you must cite in the body of the paper the author's name and the publication date of the article. The purpose of these kinds of citations is to make it easy for the reader to identify the source of an idea and locate it in the reference list at the end of the paper.

Standard Narration Citation

Here is an example of a citation that appears entirely in parentheses:

> In 1879, in Leipzig, Germany, the first formal laboratory de-
> voted to experimental psychology was founded (Hilgard,
> 1986).

Citations can also appear as part of the paper's narrative. Here is an example:

> According to Hilgard (1986), Wilhelm Wundt was probably the
> first person to refer to himself as a psychologist.

Quotations

If you are quoting directly from a source, the page number (indicated by p. for a single page and pp. for more than one page) must also be cited along with the author and year:

> As "a mechanism for governing motor activity," the brain's "primary function is essentially the transforming of sensory patterns into patterns of motor coordination" (Sperry, 1952, p. 297).

Quotations longer than 40 words should be set in an indented block without quotation marks:

> Seligman (1992) has studied optimism and draws the following conclusion:
>> People who believe good events have permanent causes try even harder after they succeed. People who see temporary reasons for good events may give up even when they succeed, believing success was a fluke. (pp. 46-47)

Note that in the case of block quotes, the page number follows the period at the end of the quote.

Secondary Citations

If you want to cite a source that you read about in another source, you can use the following format:

> Chomsky (1959), as cited by Zimbardo (1992), proposed that...

This kind of citation should be done only when the original source is truly unavailable to you and you are interpreting another interpretation of the original author.

Multiple Authors

If your source has several authors, you should cite each of them in your paper's narrative:

> Jacoby, Baker, and Brooks (1989) found picture identification to have several implications for theories of learning and theories of memory.

An ampersand (&) is used between author's names when they are enclosed in parentheses, and a semicolon separates different references:

```
Picture identification was found to have several implications
for theories of learning and theories of memory (Jacoby,
Baker, & Brooks, 1989; Smith & Clark, 1990).
```

You should list all authors the first time the citation is given, and in subsequent citations with more than two authors you may mention only the first author followed by "et al." and the date:

```
The relation of lung cancer to the exposure of tobacco smoke
is explored by Janerich et al. (1990).
```

These are the essential points of making in-text citations, but there are a couple of other situations that deserve explanation. If you are citing two works published by the same author in the same year you may designate them as a, b, c, and so on (1993a, 1993b). Alphabetical order of the works' titles determines their sequence. Also, if a work has been accepted for publication but is not yet printed you should designate it as "in press" (Hammersla, in press). If you run into other problems not answered in this section, refer to the APA *Manual*.

CONSTRUCTING THE REFERENCE LIST

A reference list is similar to a bibliography, but it only lists publications you cite in the narrative text of your paper. A bibliography, on the other hand, provides sources for further reading that are not cited in the manuscript. If you do not refer to a source within the body of your paper, do not include it in your reference list. References are placed at the conclusion of your paper on a new page. The order of the references is arranged alphabetically by the author's last name and then by date of publication. For example, an article or book would follow this format:

Authors' last names, initials. (Year of publication). Title of the article. *Journal Name, Volume Number*, Page numbers.

Authors' last names, initials. (Year of publication). *Title of the book*. (Edition or Volume number). City where publisher is located, including state abbreviation if not a major city: Publisher's name.

In the remaining portion of this section many different kinds of references are illustrated.

Journal Articles

Manning, C. A., Hall, J. L., & Gold, P. E. (1990).
Glucose effects on memory and other neuropsycholog-
ical tests in elderly humans. <u>Psychological Science, 1</u>, 307-311.

Note that only the first word of the title of the article is capitalized. You
would also capitalize the first word following a colon in a title.

Authored Book

Seligman, M. E. P. (1990). <u>Learned optimism</u>. New
York: Knopf.

Book with No Author

<u>Harper atlas of world history</u>. (1986). New York:
Harper & Row.

Edited Book

Rabkin, J. G., Gelb, L., & Lazar, J. B. (Eds.).
(1980). <u>Attitudes toward the mentally ill: Research perspectives</u>. Rockville, MD: National Institute of Mental Health.

Chapter in an Edited Book

Houghton, J. (1980). One personal experience: Be-
fore and after mental illness. In J. G. Rabkin, L.
Gelb, & J. B. Lazar (Eds.), <u>Attitudes toward the
mentally ill: Research perspectives</u> (pp. 7-14).
Rockville, MD: National Institute of Mental
Health.

Doctoral Dissertation Abstract

Massey, D. (1989). Empathy and therapeutic orientation in professional therapists and undergraduate
college students. Dissertation Abstracts International, 40, 590B.

Magazine or Newspaper Article

Fowler, R. D. (1986, May). Howard Hughes: A psychological autopsy. Psychology Today, pp. 179-184.
Goleman, D. (1985, December 17). Psychotherapy, at
100, is marked by deep divisions on approaches.
The New York Times, Section 8, pp. 1, 4.

Magazine or Newspaper Article with No Author

Psychotherapy on the ropes.   (1993, July).   The
Boston Globe, p. 34.

Paper Presented at a Meeting

Perrin, R. (1992, August). Psychosocial implications
of denominational affiliation. Paper presented at
the meeting of the American Psychological Association, Washington, DC.

Journal Article on the World Wide Web

Jacobson, J. W., Mulick, J. A., & Schwartz, A. A.
(1995). A history of facilitated communication:
Science, pseudoscience, and antiscience. American
Psychologist, 50, 750-765. Retrieved January 25,
1996,   from   the   World   Wide   Web:
http//www.apa.org/journals/jacobson.html

Newspaper Article on the World Wide Web

Sleek, S. (1996, January). Psychologists build a culture of peace. APA Monitor, pp. 1, 33 [Newspaper, selected stories on-line]. Retrieved January 25, 1996, from the World Wide Web: http//www.apa.org/monitor/peacea.html

All references from the World Wide Web begin with the same information that would be provided for a printed source (or as much of that information as possible). The Web information is then placed at the end of the reference. It is important to use "Retrieved from" and the date because documents on the Web may change in content, move, or be removed from a site altogether.

POINTS TO REMEMBER

When it comes to references, the following are a few key points often forgotten by students:

- Center the word "References" (not Bibliography) at the top of the first page of references.
- Double-space the entire reference section.
- Invert all authors' names and list them in the order they appear on the title page of the publication. Use commas to separate the authors and an ampersand (&) before the last author.
- For book titles and article titles, capitalize only the first word of the title and of the subtitle (if any) as well as proper names. Underline the volume number of a journal article and the title of the book or the name of a journal.
- Give the city of a book's publisher. If the city is not well-known or might be confused with another location, also give the state postal abbreviation.
- Give the year and month for magazine articles and the year, month, and day for newspaper articles.
- Be sure every reference you cite in your paper is included in the reference list and that the information is correct.

CHAPTER 18

TABLES AND FIGURES

SUPERSTITION is more powerful than we think. Planes flying into Tokyo International Airport never taxi up to a Gate 4 or 13. It is a matter of superstition. In Tokyo's 36-story World Trade Center, the 13th floor holds nothing but air-conditioning equipment and generators. The old section of Tokyo University Hospital has no rooms with the numbers 4 or 9. Even Japanese telephone numbers reserve the digits 42 for temporarily installed phones.

For various reasons, certain numbers can be frightening to some people. But when it comes to your experimental psychology report you should do everything you can to present numbers and statistics in ways that are clear and cause little anxiety. That is the purpose of tables and figures. They can convey a great deal of information in a succinct fashion.

TABLES

A table presents data systematically in rows and columns. It can help the reader comprehend findings in a clear way, and it can illustrate the relationships among variables that are difficult to express in the body of your writing. It is important to remember that tables are *summaries* of raw data, not the actual raw data. If your professor requires you to include your raw data, they should be placed in an appendix of your report (Rosnow & Rosnow, 1992).

For publication purposes, a table is placed on a separate page and inserted after the reference list at the end of the paper. However, for a student paper it is more convenient to place tables and figures in the text (Walvoord, 1982). Still, you should guide the reader to your table at the appropriate place in the text. For example, you can state "Transmission rates are listed in Table 1." Table numbers (e.g., Table 1, Table 2) are expressed in arabic numerals and are numbered in the order they appear. Show your readers where you would insert the table by noting it in the narrative. See Exhibit 6.

Exhibit 6 Indicating Placement of Tables

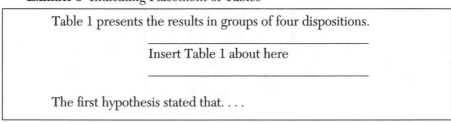

Table 1 presents the results in groups of four dispositions.

Insert Table 1 about here

The first hypothesis stated that. . . .

Each table should have a concise title that is underlined. It should appear above the table and the entire table should be double-spaced. See Exhibit 7.

Exhibit 7 Example of a Table

Table 1
Pearson Product Moment Correlations for Social
Style

Group	Empathic Concern
Adolescents	-.37*
Middle-aged adults	-.71**
Older adults	-.66***

*p < .05. **p < .01. ***p < .001

FIGURES

It is sometimes more helpful to use a figure to show a concept or statistical findings than it is to explain it in lengthy prose. A figure is any type of illustration other than a table. All charts, graphs, and illustrations are called figures.

Generally speaking, a computer with graphics capabilities is the best way of generating figures, but it is not essential. The goal is to come up with a figure that effectively communicates your information.

Each figure is numbered (e.g., *Figure 1.*) and the caption goes below the figure. See Exhibit 8.

Exhibit 8 Example of a Figure

<u>Figure 1.</u> A brief description of the figure goes here.

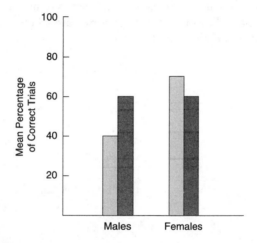

Graphs are the most common figures. Richard W. Bowen (1992) wrote a little book, *Graph It!*, to help students overcome "graphobia." He illustrates dozens of graphs and describes how to design them in detail. Here are some of the points he recommends keeping in mind:

- Information should be clearly labeled.
- Data should be plotted accurately.
- Avoid clutter.
- The predictor variable is plotted on the horizontal (x) axis.
- The criterion variable is plotted on the vertical (y) axis.
- The information on the vertical axis should progress from small to large.
- The unit of measurement should be consistent.

- The vertical axis should be about two-thirds the length of the horizontal axis.

When a paper is being prepared for publication in a journal, the figure and the figure title are placed on separate sheets of paper. In a report for a class project, however, it is generally acceptable to put the title on the same page with the figure. As with tables, figures should be numbered chronologically as they appear in the text and you should indicate where in the text the figure should be inserted.

APPENDIXES

Your instructor will probably tell you if an appendix is needed and what should be included in it. An appendix, for example, may include raw data (i.e., the subjects' original responses and scores), verbatim instructions used in the experiment, or tests administered to subjects. Appendixes are labeled with capital letters (e.g., Appendix A, Appendix B, and so on).

PART FOUR

A FEW ELEMENTS OF WRITING WELL

CHAPTER 19

THE ELEMENTS OF GRAMMAR

It is difficult to exaggerate the importance of fundamentals. Vince Lombardi, the late football strategist, was a fanatic about fundamentals. Time and again he would come back to the basic techniques of blocking and tackling. On one occasion, his team, the Green Bay Packers, lost to an inferior squad. The very next morning, Coach Lombardi called a practice. The men sat silently, having no idea what to expect from the man they feared most.

Lombardi began: "This morning we go back to the basics. . . ." Holding a football in his outstretched hand, he continued, ". . . gentlemen, *this* is a football!"

As silly as it sounds, you cannot overlook the basics. Lombardi put Green Bay, Wisconsin, on the map by emphasizing the fundamentals. He is the only coach to lead a team to three consecutive world football championships!

What works in the game of football works in the world of writing as well. The basics, or elements, of writing well include grammar, punctuation, language usage, spelling, and inclusive language. The basics do not require a lengthy discourse. The revered professor of writing William Strunk, Jr., is known for "cutting the vast tangle of English rhetoric down to size and [writing] its rules and principles on the head of a pin" (Strunk & White, 1979, p. xi). Part Four of this book is written in the "Strunkian" tradition.

The present chapter is about grammar — the rules of the English language. To succeed in your writing of psychology papers you must understand the basics of grammar. There is no way around it. Molière wrote, "To grammar even kings bow."

After a quick refresher of grammatical terms, we'll review some of the most essential grammatical rules:

- *Noun.* A person, place, thing, or idea (e.g., woman, college, psychology).
- *Proper Noun.* A particular place, person, object, or idea (e.g., Freud, Stanford).
- *Pronoun.* A substitute for a noun or proper noun (e.g., he, she, it).
- *Verb.* Action or state of being (enjoy, write).
- *Adjective.* Describes (modifies) nouns (e.g., big, new).
- *Adverb.* Describes verbs, adjectives, and other adverbs (e.g., *much* later, talked *loudly*).
- *Preposition.* Shows how a noun or pronoun is related to another word in a sentence (e.g., into, on, through).
- *Conjunction.* Joins words, phrases, or clauses (e.g., and, but, for, or).
- *Subject.* The person, object, or idea being described in a sentence (e.g., *The study of moral development* is fascinating).
- *Predicate.* The explanation of the action, condition, or effect of the subject (e.g., Counseling children *sounds like a great career*).

SUBJECT AND VERB MUST AGREE

Nouns, pronouns, and verbs are either singular or plural. If the subject noun is singular, then the verb of the sentence must also be singular. The difficulty with this rule surfaces with sentences such as this one: "According to the different theories, the development of cognitive capacities are unique to each individual." The subject of the sentence is *development*, which is singular. The verb is *are*. In this case, the sentence may "sound" fine to some ears, but the subject and verb do not agree. The noun nearest to the verb is not always the subject. An easy way of testing subject and verb agreement is to omit everything but the subject and verb. Make this a habit and be sure to avoid this common error.

A PRONOUN MUST AGREE WITH ITS ANTECEDENT

An antecedent is the noun that a pronoun replaces. If it is singular, the pronoun must be singular; if plural, the pronoun must be plural. Study this sentence: "The student can practice listening skills and watch their performance on videotape." Any problems? The subject ("student") is singular, but the pronoun ("their") is plural. You can correct this sentence by making the subject plural ("students").

BE AWARE OF VERB TENSES

Some writers use only the past tense of verbs while others try to stay in the present. Past tense is appropriate for a literature review (e.g., "researchers have shown..."). If you are writing an experimental report, the description of the procedure can be written in the past tense also (e.g., "subjects performed..."). However, your discussion of the results and your conclusions should be written in the present tense (e.g., "the data indicate..."). Use of the present tense allows your readers to join with you in deliberating the issues (APA, 1994). When you make shifts in verb tenses, the key is to do so with purpose.

PLACE MODIFIERS CLOSE TO THE WORDS THEY MODIFY

A modifier (i.e., adjective or adverb) must clearly refer to the word it is describing. Sometimes a modifier's placement in a sentence leads to ambiguity. You can eliminate any confusion by placing an adjective or an adverb as close as possible to the word it modifies. Consider this sentence: "The psychologist counseled the patients using this technique." Is the psychologist using the technique or the patients? This sentence makes it clear: "Using this technique, the psychologist counseled the patients."

UNDERSTAND HOMOPHONES

Homophones are words that are pronounced the same way but have different spellings and meanings. Students often use them incorrectly in papers. Here are a few common ones: *their, there,* and *they're*; *to, too,* and *two*; and *than* and *then*. You probably already understand the differences among them. The trick is to pay attention to them in your writing and be sure they are used correctly.

CHAPTER 20

THE ELEMENTS OF PUNCTUATION

"ALL morning I worked on the proof of one of my poems," wrote Oscar Wilde, "and I took out a comma; in the afternoon I put it back."

Dealing with things like commas, colons, and apostrophes can be an exhausting task. But punctuation is vital to effective writing. Consider these fourteen words as an example: "That that is is that that is not is not is not that it it is." Now punctuate them, and they read: That that is, is; that that is not, is not! Is not that it? It is.

Punctuation clarifies the meaning of our writing and it deserves serious attention. The following points are simple reminders of how to use punctuation correctly.

Apostrophe ('). An apostrophe is used to denote possession. To form the possessive singular or plural of nouns, add an apostrophe and *s* ('s). However, to form the possessive plural of nouns already ending with an *s*, you almost always add an apostrophe after the *s* (e.g., "The Jones' house."). A common error is to write "it's" for "its." The first is a contraction, meaning "it is." The second is a possessive.

Brackets ([ ]). Use brackets to enclose material inserted in a quotation by someone other than the quoted writer or speaker. Brackets can also enclose parenthetical material within parentheses.

Colon (:). Use a colon to introduce a list or to introduce a statement. A colon should also be used to introduce a formal or long quotation. Use a colon in noting ratios and proportions (e.g., 14:3).

Comma (,). Use a comma to separate words and phrases in a series. Use a comma before *and* and *or* in a series of three or more items. When *etc.* ends a series, it should be preceded and followed by a comma. Use a comma before and after a clause that is nonessential to the sentence. Do not use a comma to separate two independent clauses not joined by a conjunction.

Dash (—). A dash should be used to indicate an interruption in the continuity or flow of a sentence. Sometimes a pair of dashes is used instead of parentheses. Use a dash instead of the word "to" in reference to dates and pages (1950–1990; pages 44–49).

Ellipsis Dots (. . .). Ellipsis dots are used in place of omitted words or paragraphs within a quotation. A space is left before each dot and also after the last if a word follows. If an ellipsis ends a sentence it should be followed by a period (e.g., ...).

Exclamation Point (!). An exclamation point is used to mark an exclamatory word, phrase, or sentence. It is, however, rarely used in technical writing.

Parentheses ( ). Use parentheses to set off items that are structurally independent from the rest of the sentence. Parentheses are used to enclose abbreviations for previously cited items. They are also used in reference citations to enclose the date or page numbers.

Quotation Marks ("word"). Use quotation marks to enclose a direct quotation except when the quotation is long enough to be blocked (i.e., indented and set apart from the text). Quotation marks can also be used to emphasize a word or short phrase. Use quotation marks to indicate the ironic use of words. Enclose the titles of articles or speeches in quotation marks (but not periodicals or books). Use single quotation marks ('word') to enclose a quotation within a quotation.

Semicolon (;). Use a semicolon to separate two independent clauses that are not joined by a conjunction. A semicolon should also be used in lists of names with titles or addresses and in other lists that would not be clear if clauses were separated by commas.

THE ELEMENTS OF USAGE

USAGE refers to the correctness of language. William Zinsser (1980), in his wonderful book *On Writing Well*, says the guardians of usage "keep the language from becoming sloppy" (p. 42).

Using words with precision is not always easy. To help us write with care, reference books have been developed to clarify confusing words and phrases. Theodore Bernstein's *The Careful Writer: A Modern Guide to English Usage* (1965) is one of the best. In this chapter, however, I want to clarify some of the technical words psychology students most frequently misuse in their papers. Robert Sternberg (1988) provides a more detailed list of technical terms in his book *The Psychologist's Companion.*

Affect, effect. As a noun, affect is an emotion; effect is a result or outcome. As a verb, affect means to influence; effect means to accomplish.

Algorithm, heuristic. An algorithm is a systematic routine that eventually solves a problem. A heuristic is a short-cut routine for solving a problem that may or may not eventually solve the problem.

Anxiety, fear. Anxiety is a state of general apprehension. Fear is a state of apprehension in response to a specific threat.

Applied research, basic research. Applied research strives for findings of practical value. Basic research strives for findings of theoretical value, regardless of whether they have practical value.

Artificial intelligence, simulation. Artificial intelligence involves machines that optimally solve problems usually thought to require intelligence. Simulation research seeks to construct settings to elicit "natural" responses or to build machines that imitate how humans solve problems (regardless of whether the performance is optimal).

Average. Statistically, this is a synonym for *mean* (the sum of values divided by the number of values). However, to avoid confusion it is recommended that this term not be used and instead the specific central tendency terms (i.e., mean, mode, median) be used.

Avoidance learning, escape learning. Avoidance learning is motivated by avoidance of punishment (i.e., the learner is punished only if learning does not take place). Escape learning is motivated by escape from punishment (i.e., the learner is punished until learning takes place).

Capacity, ability, performance. Capacity is innate potential. Ability is how much your innate potential is developed. Neither can be truly measured. Performance is whatever is being assessed at one time.

Classical conditioning, operant conditioning. In classical conditioning, an originally neutral stimulus is repeatedly paired with a stimulus that evokes a certain response. As a result of repeated pairing, the originally neutral stimulus eventually evokes the same response. In operant conditioning, a learner operates on the environment to be rewarded.

Compulsion, obsession. A compulsion is an irresistible urge to perform a behavior repeatedly. An obsession is a recurrent thought.

Control group, experimental group. A control group does not receive the experimental treatment. An experimental group does receive the treatment.

Culture-fair test, culture-free test. A culture-fair test attempts to minimize or equalize the differential effect of different cultural experiences upon performance. A culture-free test attempts to minimize the absolute effects of any cultural experiences on performance. There is no way of knowing if a test is actually culture free.

Data, datum. The term "data" is plural. "Datum" is singular. Do not write "the data is . . ." Instead write "the data are . . ."

Deduction, induction. Deduction is reasoning from the general to the specific. Induction is inferring from the specific to the general. With induction, one can never attain certainty in one's conclusions.

Delusion, hallucination, illusion. A delusion is a false belief. A hallucination is a sensory experience in the absence of appropriate stimuli. An illusion is a misperception of a stimulus.

Dependent variable, independent variable. A dependent variable, on which the effect is measured, is dependent on the value of other variables. These other variables, which are under experimental control, are the manipulated independent variables.

Descriptive statistics, inferential statistics. Descriptive statistics summarize data (e.g., mean, median, and standard deviation). Inferential statistics provide tests of hypotheses about data (e.g., t, z, and F).

Empiricism, nativism. Empiricists see behaviors as learned primarily through experience (e.g., Skinner). Nativists claim that most behavior is innately determined (e.g., Chomsky).

Factor. This word can refer to an independent variable in an experiment. It can also refer to a mathematical representation of a hypothetical psychological construct (obtained through factor analysis).

Fixation, regression. Fixation refers to arrested development at a specific stage. Regression is returning to an earlier stage of development.

Genotype, phenotype. A genotype is a set of inherited characteristics that may or may not be overtly displayed. A phenotype is the set of characteristics that is displayed.

Identification, imitation. In identification, a person acquires the norms, values, expectations, and the social role of another person by emulating the behavior of that person. In imitation, the person mimics the behavior of another person, not necessarily acquiring the characteristics of a person's social role.

Latent content, manifest content. The latent content of a dream is its deeper, hidden meaning. Manifest content is its apparent meaning.

Learning, maturation. Learning is an increment in knowledge that occurs as a result of practice. Maturation is a behavioral change resulting from a growth process.

Mean, median, mode. The mean is the sum of a set of values divided by the number of values. The median is the middle value. The mode is the most frequently occurring value.

Neurosis, psychosis. A neurosis (although no longer "officially" used as a psychiatric catagory) is a minor disorder involving struggles with anxiety. A psychosis is a major disorder in which a person exhibits great distortions of reality.

Null hypothesis. This is often referred to as a hypothesis of no difference (e.g., treatment will produce no effect on the experimental group). It is not *no* hypothesis.

Population, sample. A population is the universe of cases to which an investigator wants to generalize results. A sample is a subset of a population and corresponds to the people in the study.

Primacy, recency. Primacy effects occur at the beginning of a sequence. Recency effects occur at the end of a sequence.

Reliability, validity. Reliability refers to how dependably a data collection technique measures something. Validity refers to how well the technique measures what it claims to measure.

Repression, suppression. Repression occurs when one's thoughts or feelings are unconsciously removed from awareness. Suppression occurs when a thought or feeling is consciously put out of one's present awareness.

Significant. A statistically significant result enables an investigator to reject a null hypothesis. Do not use the word to refer simply to any result that you think is important.

State, trait. A state is a temporary mood. A trait is a permanent disposition.

Subconscious, unconscious. The subconscious contains thoughts and feelings that are not conscious but can be brought into consciousness with little or no effort. It is sometimes called the preconscious. The unconscious contains thoughts and feelings that are difficult to bring into consciousness.

Variability, variance. Variability refers to dispersion or spread. Variance refers to a specific measure of the amount of dispersion (i.e., $\Sigma(x2)/N$, where x is the deviation of each score from the mean and N the number of cases).

CHAPTER 22

THE ELEMENTS OF SPELLING

IN 1783, Noah Webster published the *American Spelling Book*. Forty-five years later he completed his monumental *American Dictionary of the English Language*. With over 70,000 words, it was the largest English dictionary published up to that time.

Today we have hundreds of dictionaries in dozens of styles and sizes. They come as multi-volume sets, pocket-sized editions, electronic, and computerized. Regardless of its form, however, a dictionary can always be found near the student writing excellent papers. The standard spelling reference used by the American Psychological Association is *Webster's New Collegiate Dictionary*.

Here are a few guidelines to help you become an expert speller:

- Drop one *l* from prefixes and suffixes ending in *ll* when combining them with other words (e.g., always, altogether, helpful).

- For words ending in *n*, keep that letter before the suffix *ness* (e.g., suddenness, keenness).

- Omit the *e* before suffixes beginning with a vowel on words ending with a silent *e* (encouraging, lovable).

- Before adding *ing* to words ending in *ie*, you should first change the *ie* to *y* (e.g., die becomes dying).

- When words end in *s, x, ch, sh,* or *z,* the plural is formed by adding *es* to the singular (e.g., churches).

- Remember the well-known rhyme: "I before E, except after C, or when sounded as A, as in neighbor and weigh" (e.g., conceive, achieve). Here are the exceptions: counterfeit, foreign, forfeit, height, leisure, neither, seize, and weird.

- If you are writing with a word processor and it has a computerize spelling system, you are blessed. Use it!

The following is a list of words frequently misspelled in psychology term papers and research reports:

abnormality	autistic	correlation
absence	autokinetic	cost-effectiveness
accommodation	autonomy	counseling
accreditation	baccalaureate	cross-cultural
accuracy	benefited	curriculum
achievement	bureaucracy	curvilinear
adjustment	catastrophe	cyclical
administrator	centralization	defensive
adolescence	checklist	deficiency
advancement	chi-square	delusion
advisory	chimpanzee	dependence
affiliation	chromosome	depression
aggression	chronic	desensitization
aggressiveness	chronological	determinant
alcoholism	circadian	develop
alienation	classification	diagnosis
altruistic	coefficient	dialogue
ambiguity	cognitive	dilemmas
ambivalence	colloquium	discipline
amnesia	commitment	disease
analogy	committed	displacement
analysis	committee	dissonance
analytical	commodity	dominance
androgyny	communication	efficiency
anomaly	comparative	elementary
anomie	compensatory	empathize
antisocial	competence	empiricism
anxiety	compulsion	enrollment
apparatus	compulsory	environmental
apprehension	conceptualization	epistemology
archetype	conditioning	equilibrium
assimilation	consciousness	equivalence
attitude	consistent	eugenics
attribution	contiguity	existence
attrition	contingencies	existential
audiovisual	continuous	extinction
authoritarianism	cooperation	extracurricular

extrasensory
facilitation
feedback
fetishism
frequency
gender
genetic
guideline
hallucination
handicapped
helplessness
hereditary
heterogeneous
heuristic
hierarchical
holistic
homeostasis
homogeneous
hormone
hypnotism
hypothesis
hysterical
idiographic
idiosyncratic
illiteracy
illusion
ingenious
inhibition
intelligence
interdisciplinary
introversion
irradiation
juvenile
kindergarten
kinesthesia
liaison
libido
linguistic
longitudinal
luminosity
masochism

measurement
meta-analysis
methodology
milieu
mnemonics
multidimensional
multivariate
narcissistic
negativism
neonatal
neurosis
nomothetic
nonverbal
obsession
occurrence
Oedipal
operant
operationalism
optimum
orientation
overreaction
parallel
paralysis
parameter
paranoid
pedagogy
perceive
persistent
pertinent
phenomenology
precede
predominantly
probability
professional
programmed
psychiatric
psychoanalysis
psycholinguistics
psychopathology
psychosomatic
psychotic

puberty
qualitative
quantitative
questionnaire
randomized
rationalization
receive
regression
reinforcement
relevant
respondent
rhetoric
schizophrenia
self-actualization
sensitivity
separate
significance
socialization
spontaneity
statistical
stereotype
succeed
superego
symptomatology
syndrome
synthesis
taboo
tachistoscope
taxonomy
technological
testability
theoretical
therapeutic
threshold
unconscious
validity
variability
violence
voluntary
weighting
xenophobia

CHAPTER 23

THE ELEMENTS OF INCLUSIVE LANGUAGE

LANGUAGE shapes our thinking. Even when we are attempting to be conscious of avoiding stereotypes, our language can subtly convey thoughts of which we are unaware. For this reason, the *Publication Manual of the American Psychological Association* (1994) presents detailed guidelines for using inclusive language. It points out that "long-established cultural practices can exert a powerful, insidious influence over even the most conscientious author" (p. 44). Two of the most obtrusive forms of this unconscious biasing involve gender and ethnicity.

AVOIDING GENDER-BIASED LANGUAGE

Perhaps the most blatant expression of sexist language is the generic use of man. It is a striking way of ignoring females (Basow, 1992). Consider the following sentence:

```
Man is making significant strides in understanding neuro-
science.
```

Obviously, the sentence would be more accurate if it did not exclude women. The sentence, for example, can be changed to:

```
Humankind is making significant strides. . . .
```

Always avoid the use of *man* and *mankind* when you are actually talking about human beings. The use of *man* as a generic noun conveys an implicit message that women are of secondary importance.

Avoiding sexist language isn't always easy. The English language doesn't have a singular pronoun combining *he* and *she*, so a writer is often forced to make decisions regarding gender. For example, if the gender of a person you are writing about is not specified, how would you handle the following sentence?

```
When a psychologist conducts research, he/she. . . .
```

Which would you choose? There are actually several reasonable options for avoiding bias. One tactic is to alternate female and male pronouns throughout your paper or say "he or she" and "she or he." This option, however, can prove distracting to many readers. Another alternative is to rewrite sentences in a plural form:

```
When psychologists conduct research, they. . . .
```

Another option is to avoid pronouns altogether:

```
Psychologists must be patient when conducting research.
```

Sexism can also creep into writing with commonly used terms for various occupations and titles. You can avoid unnecessary gender biasing by using alternative terms. See Exhibit 9.

Exhibit 9 Nonsexist Terms

Biased	Unbiased
businessman	businessperson
chairman	chairperson
congressman	member of Congress
foreman	supervisor
fireman	fire fighter
housewife	homemaker
mailman	mail carrier
policeman	police officer
salesman	salesperson

It is also important to treat the sexes equally in your writing. For example, ask yourself if the use of adjectives describing women consistently creates a negative impression. Don't describe women in physical or sexual terms unless you are doing the same with men. Don't stereotype the sexes by always putting men in positions of authority (e.g., doctors, psychologists, administrators, etc.).

The purpose of avoiding sexist language is to become more accurate and unbiased in your writing. Careful attention to this important element of writing will become easier with time and the results are certainly worthy.

AVOIDING ETHNIC-BIASED LANGUAGE

Obvious ethnic stereotyping is easy to detect and avoid. But biases in ethnicity can also be subtle. A term such as "culturally deprived," for example, is sometimes used to refer to any group living in poverty. This description, however, does not recognize that a group may enjoy a rich cultural heritage in spite of poor economic conditions. The fact that a culture is different from the writer's does not mean it is lacking in vibrancy and ongoing tradition.

CHAPTER 24

A FINAL WORD

CAROL BURNETT, the famous comedienne, was climbing out of a cab one day in New York City. She inadvertently caught her coat in the door. As the driver continued on his way, unaware of the accident, the comedienne was obliged to run alongside the moving vehicle to avoid being pulled off her feet. A quick-thinking passerby, noticing her plight, hailed the cab and alerted the driver. Having released Ms. Burnett's coat, the driver asked her anxiously, "Are you all right?"

"Yes," she replied, still gasping for breath, "but how much more do I owe you?"

I am tempted to ask the same question, "What do I still owe you?" You have taken the time to read this book and I hope the "ride" has been worthwhile. If I knew of something more I could say to help you succeed in your writing efforts, I would say it. But now it's your turn. We have looked at a number of important pieces to the writing puzzle — paper panic, motivation, writing tools, using the library, using electronic retrieval systems, outlining, rewriting, APA style, grammar, punctuation, inclusive language, and so on. Now it is time to *just do it!*

I wish you the very best in your efforts to write excellent psychology papers. When asked how he worked, Einstein once replied, "I grope." As you write psychology papers, I hope this book will help you grope in the right direction.

Please let me know how it goes. Send correspondence to: Dr. Les Parrott, Department of Psychology, Seattle Pacific University, Seattle, Washington, 98119.

SUBMITTING A PAPER FOR PUBLICATION

Of course no writers ever forget their first acceptance. One fine day when I was seventeen I had my first, second and third, all in the same morning's mail. Oh, I'm here to tell you, dizzy with excitement is no mere phrase!

— *Truman Capote*

IF YOU write an exceptional paper that your professor believes has potential for publication in a professional journal or presentation at a professional conference, this chapter is for you. Your academic advisor or course instructor can guide you on the particulars of publishing your paper, but here are the basics of the publishing process.

Preparing and submitting a paper for publication can be time-consuming. Quality journals invest many hours in reviewing and critiquing articles. Many journals have high rates of rejection, so the process can also be stressful. If your paper is published, however, the wait and the stress can be rewarding. Making a contribution to the profession of psychology is first of all satisfying and second, it will further your professional life in numerous ways.

SELECTING A JOURNAL

The first step in submitting a paper for publication is to select an appropriate journal. A listing of many respected journals is found in Appendix B of this book. The American Psychological Association published a resource listing for authors, *Journals in Psychology* (1990), that contains editorial policies, notes on submissions, and circulation information for hundreds of different journals. For submitting an article to a more popular audience, *Magazines for Libraries* (1992) is an excellent resource.

Robert Sternberg (1988) has noted several criteria that should be considered in trying to select the best journal for your paper:

- *Quality of the journal.* Some journals are more prestigious than others. They are of the highest quality and only publish outstanding contributions. They also have very high rejection rates so the probability of publishing in them is lower. Other journals are easier to break into, but they do not carry as much weight.

- *Content of your paper.* Journal editors are looking for specific kinds of articles. They want a paper that matches their research focus (e.g., clinical or developmental), and they want a paper that follows their methodological thrust (e.g., experimental or theoretical).

- *Readership of the journal.* The quality and content of a journal influence who reads it, but the fact remains that some journals are read by many more people than are other journals. The circulation of a journal can be determined by looking through recent back issues to find the annual statement.

- *Length of your paper.* In the "information for authors" section of a journal you will often find the approximate length of articles it accepts for review. If it is not noted, examine several recent issues to discover the acceptable article length.

- *Publication lag time.* Once an article is accepted for publication it may not appear in print for as long as 18 months or more. Consider the timely nature of your paper's content and how long you are willing to wait for your paper to be published.

- *Cost of submitting your paper for review.* Most journals do not charge authors for submitting or publishing their articles. But some do. The "information for authors" section will indicate any costs involved.

- *Restrictions on authors.* A few journals publish articles by invitation only or only if you are a member of some organization. Again, the journal's "information for authors" section will indicate any such restrictions.

SUBMITTING THE PAPER

Each journal has particular editorial requirements for submission. Once you have decided on a journal, make sure your paper meets its stipulations. Generally, a paper must conform to the APA guidelines outlined in Part Three of this book. Most journals require several copies of the paper and you should also include a cover letter indicating your intention and your mailing address.

Your paper may be submitted to only one journal at a time. Simultaneous submissions are a big no, no! Send the paper initially to your first-choice journal but keep in mind your second and third choices in case your paper is rejected.

THE REVIEW PROCESS

The backbone of professional publication is a process called "peer review" or "refereeing." The majority of professional journals will send out your paper for anonymous or masked review by expert professional peers. All identifying information is removed from the manuscript. This makes the process more impartial and objective by keeping authors and reviewers unaware of each other's identities. The reviewers' job is to present a clear decision about the publishability of the paper. They will support their recommendation with a detailed, comprehensive analyses of the paper's quality and coherence (Calfee & Valencia, 1991; Stanovich, 1992).

Once all of the reviews are in (there are typically three or more reviewers), you will be notified of the article's status. Your article may be flatly accepted without having to make any revisions or it may be accepted contingent on making minor changes. On the down side, an article may be rejected outright or it may be rejected with suggestions for revisions. This allows the author to follow through on the suggestions and resubmit it, but it does not bind the editor to publish the revision.

The major reason for article rejections is lack of substance and the omission of important experimental procedures (Sternberg, 1988). Other characteristics of rejected articles include an inadequate literature review covering too much or too little; an unclear introductory section; inappropriate statistical techniques; flaws in writing style; and excessive length (Eichorn & VandenBos, 1985). If a work represents a genuine contribution to the field, however, many editors will do all they can to help an author make the paper ready for publication.

For additional pointers and a more detailed description of the publication process, I recommend William Van Til's book *Writing for Professional Publication* (1986). It is filled with many helpful suggestions and publishing tips. Another helpful piece is Robert C. Calfee and Richard R. Valencia's *APA Guide to Preparing Manuscripts for Journal Publication* (1991). You can order a copy of this booklet by writing APA Order Department, P.O. Box 2710, Hyattsville, MD, 20784.

JOURNALS
RELATED TO
PSYCHOLOGY

The following is a listing of some of the most most popular journals related to psychology. It is broadbased but not exhaustive.

Applied Psychology
Applied Psycholinguistics
Applied Psychological Measurement
Applied Psychology: An International Review
Human Relations
Journal of Applied Behavior Analysis
Journal of Applied Psychology
Journal of Applied Social Psychology
Journal of Sport and Exercise Psychology
Military Psychology
Personnel Psychology
Psychology and Marketing

Clinical Psychology
British Journal of Clinical Psychology
Child Abuse and Neglect
Clinical Psychology Review

Community Mental Health Journal
Counseling Psychologist
Journal of Abnormal Psychology
Journal of Behavior Therapy and Experimental Psychiatry
Journal of Behavioral Medicine
Journal of Consulting and Clinical Psychology
Journal of Counseling and Development
Journal of Counseling Psychology
Journal of Mental Health Counseling
Journal of Psychopathology and Behavioral Assessment
Journal of Social and Clinical Psychology
Psychological Assessment: A Journal of Consulting and Clinical Psychology
Psychotherapy: Research and Practice

Cognitive Psychology

Cognitive Neuropsychology
Cognitive Neuroscience
Cognitive Therapy and Research
Journal of Memory and Language
Perception and Psychophysics
Social Cognition
Visual Neuroscience

Communication

Applied Psycholinguistics
Brain and Language
Journal of Communication
Journal of Nonverbal Behavior
Journal of Psycholinguistic Research

Cross-Cultural

Hispanic Journal of Behavioral Science
International Journal of Behavioral Development
International Journal of Psychology
Journal of Black Psychology
Journal of Cross-Cultural Psychology

Developmental Psychology

Adolescence
British Journal of Developmental Psychology
Child Abuse and Neglect
Child Development
Cognitive Development
Development and Psychopathology
Developmental Neuropsychology
Developmental Psychobiology

Developmental Psychology
Developmental Review
Early Childhood Research Quarterly
Infant Behavior and Development
Infant Mental Health Journal
Journal of Abnormal Child Psychology
Journal of Adolescent Research
Journal of Aging and Health
Journal of Child Language
Journal of Clinical Child Psychology
Journal of Early Adolescence
Journal of Experimental Child Psychology
Journal of Pediatric Psychology
Journal of Youth and Adolescence
Monographs of the Society for Research in Child Development
Psychology and Aging

Environmental Psychology

Environment and Behavior
Journal of Environmental Psychology
Population and Environment

Experimental Psychology

Behavior Research Methods, Instruments, and Computers
Journal of Applied Behavior Analysis
Journal of Comparative Psychology
Journal of Experimental Psychology: Learning, Memory, and Cognition
Journal of Experimental Psychology: Animal Behavior Processes
Journal of Experimental Psychology: General
Journal of Experimental Psychology: Human Perception and Performance
Journal of Experimental Analysis of Behavior
Multivariate Behavioral Research
Psychometrika

Family

Family Process
Journal of Marriage and Family Therapy
Networker

General Psychology

American Journal of Psychoanalysis
American Journal of Psychology
American Psychologist

Human Sexuality

Archives of Sexual Behavior

Journal of Homosexuality
Journal of Psychology and Human Sexuality
Journal of Sex and Marital Therapy
Journal of Sex Education and Training
Journal of Sex Research

Industrial-Organizational Psychology
Human Factors
Journal of Occupational Psychology
Journal of Organizational Behavior Management

Learning
Animal Learning and Behavior
Journal of Experimental Psychology: Learning, Memory, and Cognition
Learning and Motivation

Personality and Social Psychology
Basic and Applied Social Psychology
British Journal of Social Psychology
Journal for the Theory of Social Behavior
Journal of Applied Social Psychology
Journal of Experimental Social Psychology
Journal of Personality
Journal of Personality and Social Psychology
Journal of Social and Clinical Psychology
Journal of Social and Personal Relationships
Journal of Social Issues
Journal of Social Psychology
Personality and Social Psychology Bulletin
Small Group Behavior
Social Cognition

Physiological Psychology
Animal Learning and Behavior
Archives of Clinical Neuropsychology
Behavioral and Neural Biology
Behavior Neuroscience
Biological Psychology
Brain and Cognition
Brain and Language
Cognitive Psychology
Developmental Neuropsychology
Neuropsychology
Psychobiology
Psychophysiology

Psychology of Gender
Journal of Feminist Family Therapy
Psychology of Women Quarterly
Sex Roles
Women and Therapy

Religion
The International Journal for the Psychology of Religion
Journal for the Scientific Study of Religion
Journal of Psychology and Christianity
Journal of Psychology and Judaism
Journal of Psychology and Theology
Journal of Pastoral Psychotherapy
Pastoral Psychology
Zygon

School Psychology
Journal of Instructional Psychology
Journal of School Psychology
Professional School Psychology
Psychology in the Schools
School Psychology Review
Teaching of Psychology

Treatment
Addictive Behaviors
Behavior Modification
Behavior Therapy
Behavioral Residential Treatment
Biofeedback and Self-Regulation
Contemporary Psychoanalysis
Counseling Psychologist
Family Therapy
Individual Psychology
Issues in Ego Psychology
Journal of Anxiety Disorders
Journal of Behavioral Medicine
Journal of Integrative and Eclectic Psychotherapy
Journal of Psychotherapy and the Family
Journal of Reality Therapy
Person-centered Review
Psychoanalytic Psychology
Transactional Analysis Journal
Violence and Victims

REFERENCES

American Psychological Association (1994). *Publication manual of the American Psychological Association* (4th ed.). Washington, DC: Author.

American Psychological Association (1990). *Journals in psychology* (3rd ed.). Washington, DC: Author.

American Psychological Association (1991). *Thesaurus of psychological index terms* (6th ed.). Washington, DC: Author.

American Psychological Association (1992). *PsychLIT Quick Reference Guide*. Wasington DC: Author.

American Psychological Association (n.d.). *Searching PsycLIT on CD-ROM*. Washington, DC: Author.

Basow, S. A. (1992). *Gender: Stereotypes and roles* (3rd ed.). Pacific Grove, CA: Brooks/Cole.

Bernstein, T. M. (1965). *The careful writer: A modern guide to English usage*. New York: Atheneum.

Bostain, R., & Robbins, A. (1990). Effective instruction for searching CD-ROM indexes. *Laserdisk Professional, 3*(1), 14–17.

Bowen, R. W. (1992). *Graph it!: How to make, read, and interpret graphs*. New York: Prentice-Hall.

Calfee, R. C., & Valencia, R. R. (1991). *APA guide to preparing manuscripts for journal publication*. Washington, DC: American Psychological Association.

Cameron, L., & Hart, J. (1992). Assessment of PsycLIT competence, attitudes, and instructional methods. *Teaching of Psychology, 19,* 239–242.

Eichorn, D. H., & VandenBos, G. R. (1985). Dissemination of scientific and professional knowledge: Journal publication within APA. *American Psychologist, 40,* 1309–1316.

Goleman, D. (1995). *Emotional intelligence.* New York: Bantam.

Howard, W. A., & Barton, J. H. (1986). *Thinking on paper.* New York: Morrow.

Hubbuch, S. M. (1985). *Writing research papers across the curriculum.* New York: Holt, Rinehart and Winston.

Katz, B., & Katz, L. S. (1992). *Magazines for libraries.* New Providence, NJ: R. R. Bowker.

Klauser, H. A. (1987). *Writing on both sides of the brain: Breakthrough techniques for people who write.* San Francisco: Harper & Row.

McCormick, M. (1971). *The New York Times guide to reference materials* (rev. ed.). New York: Signet.

Reed, J. G., & Baxter, P. M. (1983). *Library use: A handbook for psychology.* Washington, DC: American Psychological Association.

Rosnow, R. L., & Rosnow, M. (1992). *Writing papers in psychology* (2nd ed.). Belmont, CA: Wadsworth.

Schmitt, D. E. (1992). *The winning edge: Maximizing success in college.* New York: HarperCollins.

Schultz, D. (Ed.). (1990). *Tools of the writer's trade.* New York: HarperCollins.

Schultz, K., & Salomon, K. (1990, February 1). End users respond to CD-ROM. *Library Journal,* pp. 56–57.

Seligman, M. E. P. (1990). *Learned optimism.* New York: Knopf.

Silver Platter Information. *PsycLIT Quick Reference Guide* (1992). Wellesley Hills, MA: Author.

Stanovich, K. E. (1992). *How to think straight about psychology* (3rd ed.). New York: Addison Wesley Longman.

Sternberg, R. J. (1988). *The psychologist's companion: A guide to scientific writing for students and researchers* (2nd ed.). New York: Cambridge University Press.

Stock, M. (1985). *A practical guide to graduate research.* New York: McGraw-Hill.

Strunk, W., Jr., & White, E. B. (1979). *The elements of style* (3rd ed.). New York: Macmillan.

Van Til, W. (1986). *Writing for professional publication* (2nd ed.). Boston: Allyn and Bacon.

Walter, T., & Siebert, A. (1990). *Student success: How to succeed in college and still have time for your friends* (5th ed.). Fort Worth, TX: Holt, Rinehart and Winston.

Walvoord, B. E. (1982). *Helping students write well: A guide for teachers in all disciplines*. New York: The Modern Language Association of America.

Zinsser, W. (1990). *On writing well: An informal guide to writing nonfiction* (4th ed.). New York: HarperCollins.

INDEX